Guns and Gunmaking Tool of Southern Appalachia

The Story of the Kentucky Rifle

Second Edition

By
John Rice Irwin

Ed Sherwood, a long-time fixture at the Museum of Appalachia, is shown here working on a walnut gunstock in the McClung House. The flintlock over the fireplace is typical of the early mountain-made rifles of this region. (Photo by Gary Hamilton)

Dedicated to the old-time mountain gunsmith whose engineering brilliance was combined with his artistic talents to produce not only his most important, but also his most beautiful possession.

ACKNOWLEDGEMENTS

I am indebted to a number of kind and knowledgeable people for their assistance in connection with the writing and compilation of this book: Frank Hoffman who is responsible for the photographs not otherwise credited; Dr. Frances Morgan for her grammatical suggestions; my expert friends, David Byrd, Everett Smith, Chuck Sharp, and Clarence Runtsch, for their advice and suggestions; Joe Diehl and Gene Purcell for their information relative to the early mountain hunters and gunmakers; Betty Martin Thompson and her husband, Charles, for their many acts of assistance in connection with gathering information and relics relative to her father, gunmaker Hacker Martin; Eliot Wigginton and Ed Trout for providing photographs; the gunmaking Sloans of Monroe County, Tennessee; my wife, Elizabeth, for protecting me from the telephone while I labored over the volume; Selma Shapiro and Jack Crouch for their reading of the manuscript; Robert Cornet, who, as director of the Appalachian Development Center at Morehead State University has assisted in the publication of the work; and finally Audrey Prince for her varied acts of assistance. And I am grateful to countless numbers of my mountain friends who have inspired and informed me over the years relative to the guns and gunmakers of our Southern Appalachian Mountains.

Table of Contents

INTRODUCTION

I think that no people developed more affinity for and dependence upon the rifle than did those early pioneers who settled in this expansive yet ill-defined region referred to as the Southern Appalachian Mountains. (It is roughly an area now comprising Eastern Kentucky, Southwest Virginia, Western North Carolina, all of East Tennessee, and Northeast Georgia -- others would include parts of other states.)

The first settlers in this region, like the traders, trappers, hunters, and explorers before them, would no more have entered into this wilderness without their rifles than they would have gone into battle unarmed. And it wasn't long before quaint and often pitifully inadequate little gunmaker shops appeared, along with the scant tools and equipment for making the graceful and serviceable weapons which came to be known internationally as the American rifle, nationally as the Kentucky rifle, but which was called locally "the squirrel rifle" or the "hog rifle." And, in this writer's opinion, it became and remains the most popular and most sought after collector weapon in the country.

For a quarter century I have traversed the picturesque hills and hollows of this area in search of tools of the mountain riflemakers, and I have acquired virtually all that I have found. The purpose of this simple treatise is to record as much information as possible relative to these rifles, the gunmaking tools, and the people involved. Nothing more. It is felt that an object is infinitely more interesting and important if its history is known: the man who made it; the intended purpose of the item; the geographical area of its origin; its approximate age and so forth.

These items, along with a number of early rifles and crossbows, are now on display in the Museum of Appalachia which I started as an endeavor to depict the culture and lifestyle of these resourceful and noble people.

In addition to the gun display, the Museum, which is located fifteen miles north of Knoxville, Tennessee, on I-75 at Norris, features forty other exhibits and over thirty completely furnished log structures in a seventy-five acre frontier-type setting. The Museum is open during daylight hours the year 'round.

J.R.I.

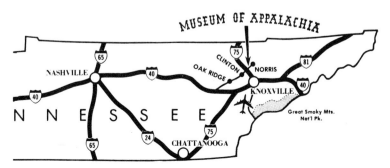

THE KENTUCKY RIFLE, ITS DEVELOPMENT AND USE

Chapter I

Lancaster County, Pennsylvania is considered to be the birthplace of the Kentucky rifle. From that area, thousands of men set out to explore (and eventually settle) the great wilderness to the west and southwest -- Virginia, Tennessee and Kentucky. Possibly because Kentucky was the most remote, it came to be more closely identified with the frontier for which the rifle was so necessary. A person going into Kentucky would surely require a rifle -- hence, the possible reason this long-barreled, full-stocked, graceful weapon came to be known as the Kentucky rifle. My friend, Eliot Wigginton, the man who started the world-famous "Foxfire" project, states that the American flintlock came to be known as the Kentucky rifle "because it was called that in the extremely popular ballad, *The Hunters of Kentucky,* written about the Battle of New Orleans." The specific allusion is as follows:

"Jackson he was wide awake and not afraid of trifles
For he knew what aim we take, with our Kentucky rifles"

(This battle between Jackson's untrained men from the Appalachian region of Tennessee, Kentucky, the surrounding area, and the polished British soldiers resulted in what is probably the most one-sided victory (or defeat) in the history of warfare. The British had 700 killed and the Americans only 7. Interestingly, and unknown to either side, the war had ended two weeks before the battle was fought.)

The Kentucky rifle's ancestor was the German and Austrian Jaeger rifle, but it is different from its European counterpart in that it has a much longer barrel with sights set further apart which contributes to improved accuracy. Also, the Kentucky rifle is generally of a smaller caliber requiring less lead and powder, a most important factor to a frontiersman who was usually a great distance from his source of supply. The stock of the Kentucky rifle is considerably more graceful in appearance and has the added quality of ease in handling as compared to the shorter, clumsy European rifle of the same and previous periods.

The rifle takes its name from a series of spiral grooves, called rifles, cut inside the barrel so as to cause the bullet to assume a spinning motion as it exits the muzzle. This enables the projectile to travel in a much straighter direction than a bullet fired from a smooth bore weapon.

Although virtually every settler carried the rifle with him, he could not replace it on the frontier once it became inoperable. Nor could the growing number of sons and grandsons of these pioneers spend many months journeying back East for their weapons. Hence, numerous part-time gunsmiths emerged throughout the new territory. The guns made in these crude shops, though often very accurate, were easily distinguished from those made in Pennsylvania. Instead of ornate and decorated stocks of curly maple, they were plain, simple and most always of walnut. Whereas the Pennsylvania rifles featured brass hardware, those made in Tennessee and North Carolina were forged of iron. Also, the frontier pieces did not have the engraved patch boxes and the inlaid German silver figures that were common on those made in Pennsylvania.

Authorities on "Kentucky" rifles can often tell at a glance whether the rifle was made in East Tennessee, North Carolina, Maryland, Pennsylvania, or Virginia. But to the untrained observer, they look very similar. Relatively few guns made in the Southern Appalachians were "signed" by the maker, though he took great pride in his workmanship.

My great, great grandfather, George Rice, for example, was a riflemaker of local renown. But as most craftsmen of this region, he had other interests such as farming, blacksmithing, milling, etc. On display in the Museum are three rifles reputed to have been made by George Rice or his father, James. Henry Rice, grandfather of George, received a land grant, dated September 12, 1787, for 640 acres of land in what became to be known as Big Valley in Union County, Tennessee, some fifteen miles northeast of the Museum. According to the late W.D. Thomas, who was this area's most renowned historian, George Rice, along with his brother-in-law, George Snodderly, built a gunshop on Lost Creek, a mile from where his father built the now famous wooden-geared water mill in 1798.

A dam was built across the creek for storing water to power an annealing process for making steel for the rifles, according to Thomas. The big trip hammer, or helve hammer, weighing several hundred pounds, was taken to the old Rice Mill after the gunshop was closed, and was moved to a site near Norris Dam in 1936 when the site of the original mill was covered by the first TVA lake. It sat beside the door of the old mill for years, until it was acquired by the Smithsonian Institution in Washington.

The early Kentucky rifles were of the flintlock type, requiring a mechanism which struck a piece of flint against a steel plate called a frizzen, or battery, providing a spark of fire which ignited the powder in the pan, which in turn fired the powder inside the barrel. (This technique was developed by the French in the early 1600's.) Early in the 1800's the percussion cap was invented and soon thereafter most of the Kentucky rifles were converted to the cap-and-ball type. After about 1830-1840 most Kentucky rifles were made using the percussion (cap-and-ball) ignition system.

Although the metal cartridges were coming into use nationally in the late 1850's, the muzzle loader remained in use, and was still being made in the mountains of this region into the late 19th Century and even into the early part of this century. But there were relatively few gunmakers, and once the factory-made guns became available, the limited equipment disappeared rapidly even though the rifles remained in comparative abundance.

One must understand that even though there are hundreds of tools usually employed in the various processes of making rifles, the average mountain gunmaker may have owned only a handful, most, if not all, of which he had to make for himself.

The tools of Will Howell, who lived on Flat Top Mountain in North Carolina, are a good example. This old gentleman made not only all the tools necessary for making a complete rifle, but he also made the tools needed to make the tools. He made screw plates and screw taps for threading the screws, bolts, various tools for cutting steel, assorted carving tools, a bowdrill, etc. He had a total of seventy-six tools, all of which he made, and all from old files, rasps, and other scrap metal. David Byrd of Erwin, Tennessee, who lives about twenty-five miles from the home of Will Howell, acquired this very rare collection from the Howell family; and many years later I bought it from him. They are now a part of the rifle collection display at the Museum.

Even after the homestead was well established and hunting was not so important, the rifle was used to kill the hogs, which provided the most staple meat in the region. They often ran wild and could only be brought down with the accurate rifle. As stated earlier the Kentucky rifle was most commonly referred to in our area as the "hog" rifle. When I was a child, I never heard it called anything except the "old hog rifle" or sometimes the "squirrel gun". I never heard the 'old folks' use the term "Kentucky rifle."

But my longtime friend, Dow Weaver from Erie in neighboring Roane County, has a different theory as to why this weapon came to be called the hog rifle in Southern Appalachia. In one of his letters to me he states:

"After Ferguson was killed in the Battle of King's Mountain and the British surrendered, the Tennessee mountain men came out from behind the bushes and logs and rocks and one of the British officers exclaimed, 'What a hog of a rifle you fellow got', and that was where the hog rifle got its name. Now, I know they are called Pennsylvania or Kentucky rifles elsewhere, but in Western North Carolina and North Georgia and East Tennessee, they are hog rifles."

The following descriptions of gunmaking artifacts, along with their regional history, as I know it, hopefully will help us to appreciate the long and laborious process required to produce the famous Kentucky rifle which played such an important part in the development of this country.

When Alfred Stooksbury of nearby Raccoon Valley in Union County sold this gun, shown at the bottom, to Kenneth Keck he wrote and signed the following letter which is still attached to the stock:

"To Whom It May Concern"

April 1, 1966

I, Alfred Stooksbury, sell this hog rifle to Kenneth Carl Keck-- this rifle is a dark pineapple stock (full stock) this gun is approximately a 38 caliber. This rifle belonged to my grandfather Alfred Boy Bledsoe. He was born, according to a biblical record, October 23, 1853 - died December 3, 1928. It is said that Grandfather purchased this rifle from Albert Nelson. I am 67 years old at this time and shot the gun when I was a boy of 15-16 years of age. This gun is thought to be 125 or more years old. Selling price $100.00.

(signed) Alfred Stooksbury

There are several interesting features of this gun. First, it has the open tallow hole in the stock, a characteristic of the rifles made by my great, great, grandfather, George Rice. Since the Stooksburys, Bledsoes, and Nelsons lived near the old Rice place in Union County, and since it resembles the Rice guns in several ways, I feel that it was made by George Rice. If Alfred is correct in his dating of the rifle, it was made in the early 1840's, a time when George was in his prime — about 50 years of age.

Another unusual feature of the gun is the folk art carving, or checks, cut into the stock. I would seriously doubt that the maker of the rifle did this -- tradition has it that the simple carving was the work of one who sat in the forest waiting for a squirrel.

This full-stock rifle shown in the center of the photograph is made of walnut as are all those shown above. With all iron hardware, it is a typical Southern Appalachian "hog" rifle. It was signed by the maker "J.G." Note the unusual lead inlay gracing and protecting the muzzle end of the stock. The end of the barrel has seven tiny indentations surrounding the bore -- possibly the maker's identification or trademark.

The cap-and-ball rifle shown in the top of the photograph belonged to the Hodge family of the Ball Camp section of Knox County, Tennessee, some twenty miles from the Museum. I also acquired it from Kenneth Keck (a brother-in-law of Congressman John Duncan) of Knoxville. It is signed, but I can 'make out' only the letter "R" -- or is it a "K"?

9

Bledsoe-Stooksbury rifle close-up showing checked stock decoration.

ALFRED "BOY" BLEDSOE HOME

This was the log home, located on Clear Creek in Union County, of Alfred "Boy" Bledsoe, owner of the rifle described on the previous page. It was reportedly built by William Bridges.

The chimney is obviously a replacement of the original, which I surmise must have been of the "stick and mud" type because of the unusual overhang. This would have prevented the mud from being washed out by the rain. A stone or brick chimney would need no such protection. (Photo about 1935 by Marshall Wilson)

EARLY FLINTLOCK RIFLE

The writer is shown here with an early, and unusually long flintlock-type Kentucky rifle. The barrel bears a thousand marks of the hammer that was used to forge it, as does the trigger guard and other hardware attachments. The rifle has a barrel 53-1/2 inches in length, and a bore which is approximately 50 caliber. It is in firing condition having been last fired at the Museum in commemoration of the Bicentennial.

According to Everett Smith, from whom it was purchased, this flintlock was first acquired from Hawkins County in upper East Tennessee, one of the first sections of the state to be settled by the Whites.

TYPICAL APPALACHIAN RIFLES

Much of the gunmaking equipment in this exhibit came from the Sloan family of Notchie in Monroe County, Tennessee, and will be discussed later in connection with the gunboring machine. This Kentucky cap-and-ball rifle shown at the top of the photograph came from that area. It is signed on the barrel "T.S." and is believed to have been made by the Sloans using this equipment. But this cannot be documented. The cap-and-ball rifle replaced the flintlock in the early 1880's and is so called because of the round ball which it fires and because of the percussion cap which the hammer strikes to ignite the powder.

This simple, almost crude, rifle was typical of the Tennessee mountain-made gun   there is no silver inlay, no patch box, and all the hardware is iron except the trigger guard, which is brass. It is a "half-stock" so called because the stock does not extend the full length of the barrel. It was acquired from my cousin, Chuck Sharp, of Lenior City, Tennessee.

The rifle at center is more fancy than the typical Appalachian-made gun with its brass butt plate, trigger guard, and patch box; but it nevertheless lacks all of the ornate features of a Pennsylvania or "up-East" rifle. It was acquired from Everett Smith near Friendsville, Blount County, Tennessee, and he acquired it from that area; but its exact origin is unknown.

The patch box was used to carry small pre-cut patches for wrapping the bullet so it would fit snugly in the bore of the rifle;

and it was used for storing tallow for greasing the bullet so it could more easily be forced into position. The patch box is opened by using the thumb nail.

Virtually all of the Pennsylvania rifles had patch boxes, but most of those made in this region did not. If they did, they were often of iron -- and some merely had a hole bored in the stock for tallow with no covering at all, as is the case of some rifles pictured on the following pages.

One of the most crudely made rifles I have seen, the weapon shown in the bottom photograph, could nevertheless be quite accurate. The mountain gunsmith had two primary goals in mind when he made a rifle; first, it had to be accurate; and secondly, it needed to be durable and sturdy. It was never characteristic for the people of this region to be "fancy" or "frilly" in the making of guns, furniture, iron items, or anything else.

This gun also was purchased from Chuck Sharp, mentioned earlier, and is from the East Tennessee area - but it had been "traded around" so that its origin is unknown. It is signed on the left side of the stock "G.E.P." and is dated 1871. It is possible that these initials and the corresponding date were inscribed by the gun's owner and not its maker. This type rifle was made in the mountains of this region long after the more modern cartridge type weapons came into popular usage in other parts of the country.

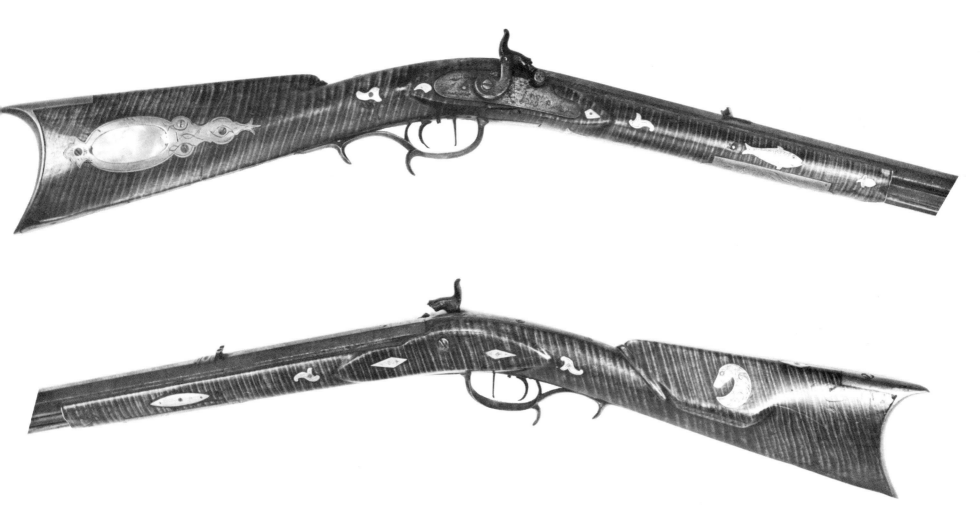

JOHN LAIR RIFLE

This highly decorated, curly maple stock rifle stands in direct contrast to the typical Appalachian mountain gun. Although it was bought in Renfro, Kentucky, from John Lair, founder of the nationally famous Renfro Valley Barn Dance, the rifle was likely made in Pennsylvania or Ohio, and "imported" perhaps at an early date, into Appalachia.

HACKER MARTIN PISTOL

One of the best known old time gunmakers in America to practice the art in this century was the legendary Hacker Martin of Cedar Creek, near Jonesboro, the state's oldest town. A descendant from early pioneer stock (including the Kefauvers), Hacker developed an early interest in guns from his gunmaking grandfather Martin, and he made his first gunstock at the age of 14 out of a walnut post from his grandfather's porch.

Hacker's fame as a master gunmaker spread throughout the country, and his ancient cornmill, which also served as his gunshop, was sought out by hundreds seeking expert repair for their weapons or hoping to buy one of his famous weapons. Robert Scott Carr, Jr. writing in the 1965 October issue of *Muzzle Blasts* said: "Those who knew Hacker and visited him in his shop admire him as the last of the only true artists America ever produced the makers of the Kentucky Rifle."

In 1970 Ogilvie H. Davis, in an article carried in the July-August edition of *Muzzle Blasts* declared that "Most every collector of note in the country today has a rifle either by Hacker Martin or Lester Smith." Lester Smith was one of Hacker's most famous students.

After the old-time gunmakers had passed on, and before the national revival of this art, there was a period of time during which the link was almost lost. Hacker Martin, perhaps as much as any other person, helped to carry the old ways across the chasm until it was safely in the hands of the thousands of modern enthusiasts, and is, hopefully, forever retrieved from the world of lost art.

In the section on Gunmaking in the recently published *Foxfire Five* book, eighteen pages were devoted to Hacker Martin. Turner Kirkland of Jackson, Tennessee, probably the nation's best-known guntrader, said of him: "Hacker started making rifles in the 1920's. He never made what you'd call a reproduction. His rifles were a continuation of the hand production as they were done before..."

Earl Lanning, the gunsmith from Waynesboro, North Carolina, is quoted by *Foxfire Five* as saying "Hacker Martin was a true gunsmith if there ever was one in the world."

Those who knew him often commented on Hacker's dry wit and sage sayings. When he was asked the inevitable question of how long it took him to make a gun, he replied: "From three days to six months, depending on what sort of rifle you want to make up."

The flintlock pistol shown here is typical of those made by Hacker, virtually every part having been made from "scratch" and by using the old type tools which he made from various scraps of metal. The brass buttplate, the trigger guard, and other parts still bear the marks of the hammer where they were slowly shaped into the graceful forms -- even the screws were handmade by Hacker. I purchased this pistol from David Byrd, my guntrader-collector friend from Erwin, Tennessee, mentioned earlier. Part of the tools used to make this and other guns are pictured and discussed in Chapter V. I recently acquired them from Hacker's old gunshop, from his daughter Betty Thompson.

The legendary Hacker Martin standing in the doorway of his newly completed gunshop (Photograph courtesy of Hacker's daughter, Betty Martin Thompson)

UNCLE RUFIE RICE

Uncle Rufie is shown here at his springhouse in 1935 with two Kentucky rifles made by his grandfather, George Rice (1784-1868). J. Rufus Rice, my great uncle, was a farmer, businessman, inventor, operator of the famous Rice Grist Mill for over 50 years, and friend of President Teddy Rosevelt, having worked with him on a ranch in Montana. These rifles, originally of the flintlock type, were converted to the cap-and-ball by Uncle Rufie's father, Henry Rice. (Photo about 1935 by Marshall Wilson)

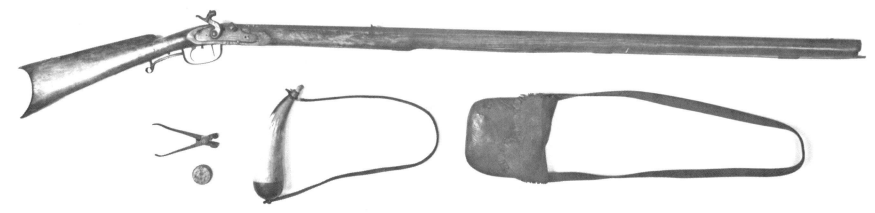

JAMES RICE RIFLE

    This rifle, according to the following documentation, was made by James Rice, great grandfather of Uncle Rufie and my great, great, great, grandfather. James Rice settled in Big Valley, some 20 miles from the Museum, about 1787, one of the thirteen children of old Henry Rice. He soon built the wooden cog and gearing cornmill (1798) which is still in operation near Norris Dam, four miles northwest of the Museum.

    I first heard that one Cowan Hood, Jr. of Knoxville had a rifle that was made by my ancestor; but upon investigation I found that he had sold it to Kevin Pipes of Blount County. It was after much negotiation that I purchased the rifle from Pipes.

    Mr. Hood acquired the rifle from Asbury Wilson, a well-known citizen of Maynardville, county seat of Union County where the Rices lived. In a letter to Kevin Pipes, Mr. Hood states:

    "This is an early pioneer rifle made by gunsmith James Rice. He was the gunsmith and operator of the Lost Creek Gristmill built in 1798. Rice made a good number of flintlock rifles and shotguns for settlers in Tennessee and Kentucky.

This rifle was originally a flintlock and was probably made during the early 1800's -- it was later converted to percussion when such firearms came into use. It was in the possession of Asbury Wilson of Maynardville who presented it to Cowan Hood, Jr. in 1933."

Best Wishes

Signed: C. Hood, Jr.

    All the metal is iron and all shop made except the lock which was made by the Conestoga rifle works. The powder horn, bullet molds, and pouch came with the gun.

GEORGE RICE RIFLE

The rifle shown here, according to tradition, was made by my great, great grandfather, George Rice, discussed earlier. George was a farmer and operator of the old mill from 1829-1868, as well as a gunmaker. When I was a child I heard stories indicating that George Rice "couldn't be beat" when it came to making rifles. And my Grandfather Irwin said that he had often heard the old folks say that George Rice could "hit a bullet hole at fifty yards." There was a rule, so I have often heard, that George Rice's guns were not allowed in local shooting matches because of their superior accuracy.

This rifle came into the possession of Annie Rice, daughter of George. She married George Woods and they reared their family in a large log house which still stands four miles east of the Museum. It was passed down to Ed Woods, and later to his daughter, Christine Woods Wallace, who made it available to the Museum.

The horn, molds and pouch had been with the rifle for as far back as anyone in the Woods family could remember. The horn has the letters "R.W." which could be the initials of Robert Woods, son of George and brother of Ed.

RICE RIFLES

My brother David Irwin holds a rifle (at left) made by our great, great, great grandfather, James Rice, on the Tennessee frontier in Big Valley. (Note the two open tallow holes in the stock.) The rifle shown at right belonged to our grandfather, Marcellus Moss Rice.

17

RICE-SNODDERLY RIFLE

I discovered this early mountain rifle recently in an old home in nearby Racoon Valley and was immediately impressed by its similarity to the Rice made guns. After a few inquiries, I learned that the family who had owned the gun came from Union County, and that their closest neighbor was old Henry Snodderly, the gunmaker who lived on Hinds Creek. (He is discussed at some length in Chapter IV in connection with the rifle guides.) The Snodderlys and Rices had intermarried and at one time jointly operated a gunshop. Because of these circumstances, and because of the gun's style, I feel that it is reasonable to assume that this rifle was made by the Snodderlys or the Rices, or possibly by George Rice and George Snodderly, brothers-in-law, who worked together for a period of time.

The walnut stock, the iron hardware, and especially the open tallow hole, rare even in this area, were all characteristic of the Rice guns. The brass decoration was probably affixed later. (Photo by the author)

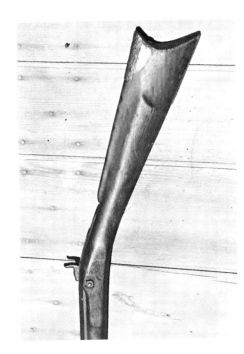

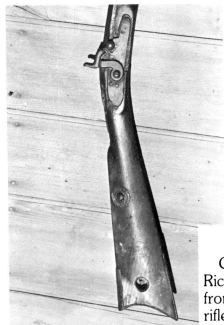

CHUCK SHARP, GUNSMITH

Chuck Sharp, great, great, great grandson of gunmaker James Rice, is shown here at the Museum with a rifle he had just made from "scratch". It is of the same style and design as the James Rice rifle shown on a previous page. Chuck, who has been a great Kentucky rifle enthusiast all his life, was reared in adjoining Knox County and now resides in Birmingham. (Photo by the author)

18

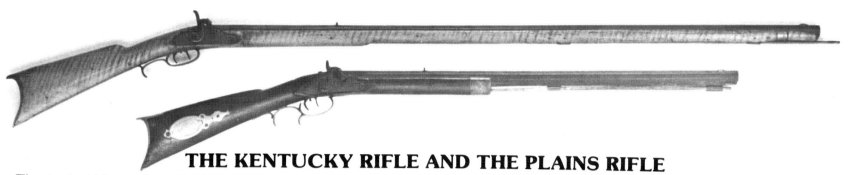

THE KENTUCKY RIFLE AND THE PLAINS RIFLE

The typical Kentucky rifle shown in the top of the photograph was long, graceful, and exceptionally accurate. The so-called plains rifle, shown in the bottom of the photograph, was shorter, heavier built, and could be carried much easier by a man on horseback. Although not as accurate, nor as attractive, it was more practical for those settlers moving into the midwest in the 1830's and 1840's.

The long rifle with the tiger-stripe maple stock has an inscription on the top of the barrel as follows: "Lancaster, PA. - Warranted". The plains rifle has no markings. I acquired both pieces from my friend, Fred Carter, who has the Cumberland Museum in the mountain town of Clintwood, near the Kentucky line in southwestern Virginia.

JAKE SEIVER RIFLE

This most typical Tennessee gun belonged to Jake Seiver who lived in the "upper end" of Dutch Valley near Lake City and only eight miles west of the Museum. The stock is walnut, the hardware is handmade iron, and there is no inlay. It was purchased from the heirs of Jake; and, according to information they supplied me, it had belonged to Jake's grandfather. The Seivers were early settlers in that area, and there are hundreds of their descendants in the county today. (Photo by the author)

D.T. PEDEN RIFLE

This rifle is signed "D.T. Peden," a gunmaker who made rifles in the Greeneville, South Carolina area during the Revolutionary War period. Some early settlers in this East Tennessee region came through that region; and perhaps it was brought into this area at an early date. It is another weapon acquired from David Byrd on the Tennessee-North Carolina border near Johnson City, Tennessee.

WILLIAM BEALS RIFLE

William Beals' gunshop was on the rugged banks of the Nolichucky River at the mouth of the California Branch and near a place locally called "the Devil's Looking Glass" about two miles northwest of the town of Erwin, Tennessee, on the North Carolina border. Beals was a carpenter, cabinetmaker, and blacksmith, as well as a gunsmith. His shop was eventually washed away by the wild Nolichucky and even the heavy anvil was forever lost.

William (1821-1898) was the son of John Beals who was born in 1801 and died in 1855. John was paying taxes on this land on the Nolichucky in 1821, as documented by a receipt in the possession of David Byrd. William Beals had some sons who were gunmakers, and one of those sons, William Beals, Jr., according to local historians, was the last man hanged in Erwin, county seat of Unicoi County.

This rifle, which bears Beals' name on the barrel, has a walnut stock, and all the hardware except the lock was apparently handmade by Beals. It was purchased from David Byrd who lives near Beals' old gunshop.

GUNMAKER WILLIAM BEALS OF ERWIN, TENNESSEE

(Photo courtesy of David Byrd)

AMBROSE LOVING (LAWING) RIFLE

Ambrose Loving (sometimes spelled Lawing) is pictured here in his log dirt-floored shop with two of the rifles he made. According to oral tradition, Loving rifles were considered to be of superior quality and commanded a price of $7.00 each, while the usual price for such weapons was only $5.00.

Loving served as a private in McInturff's Company, 2nd North Carolina Mounted Infantry, during the Civil War. He had settled in Flag Pond in 1860, just before the war started, and presumably became acquainted with McInturff there. The village of Flag Pond, originally called Floypond, had only one school and three stores in the 1880's, according to Goodspeed, the noted Tennessee historian. (Photo courtesy of David Byrd)

UNICOI COUNTY RIFLES

The tiny mountain county of Unicoi, located in the extreme northeast corner of Tennessee, on the North Carolina border, seems to have produced an inordinate number of gunsmiths. It is a rugged county, once described by Goodspeed, one of the state's foremost early historians, as having little land suitable for cultivation. The fact that hunting was a primary means of obtaining food may explain the emphasis upon the rifle. And, of course, no one would have felt safe without a gun in the house.

William Lewis, one of the county's first settlers (on Indian Creek), was killed by Indians along with his wife and seven children, according to Goodspeed. One son escaped and a daughter was taken captive and was returned to the White settlement in exchange for one locally made rifle. (Interestingly, Unicoi, and more particularly its county seat of Erwin, is receiving current world attention in connection with the missing "weapon-grade" uranium at the local nuclear plant.)

The three rifles shown here were made by Bean, Harris and McInturff respectively, and are a part of the David Byrd collection along with the Loving rifle on the previous page. The similarities of the cheekrest and of other features is understandable in that they were made within a few miles of one another during the same general period of time.

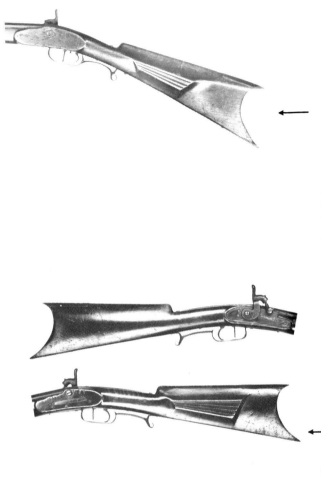

L.W. McINTURFF RIFLE

Captain L.W. McInturff, who formed and commanded a company for the Union during the Civil War, made rifles at various locations in Unicoi County. His style, it will be noted, is the most different of the four shown. (Photo courtesy of David Byrd)

CHARLES BEAN RIFLE

The Bean family is easily the best known of the early Tennessee gunmakers. Captain William Bean, a friend and compatriot of Daniel Boone, was one of the state's earliest settlers (1769); and his son Russell was, according to all the early historians, the first White child born in what is now the state of Tennessee.

Several Beans made rifles, (Hacker Martin said six generations). The relationship of Charles Bean, who made and signed this one, to the other gunmakers by the same name is unknown to the writer. His shop was located at a place called Shallow Ford on the Indian Creek some three miles south of Erwin, and only a few miles north of Flag Pond where Loving's shop was located. The rifle is believed to have been made in the 1880's. (Photo courtesy of David Byrd).

← JASON L. HARRIS RIFLE

This fine curly maple rifle was made by Jason Harris in the community of Flag Pond before the Civil War and before Loving opened his shop there. Harris, who was a Union soldier, was killed during the War at Marshall, North Carolina. (Photo courtesy of David Byrd)

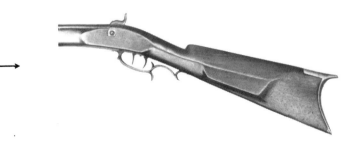

FLINTLOCK RIFLE

This flintlock was purchased from David Byrd and is signed on the barrel: "H.N.B." Although it cannot be documented, Byrd and I think this rifle was made by the famous gunmaking Bean family discussed earlier.

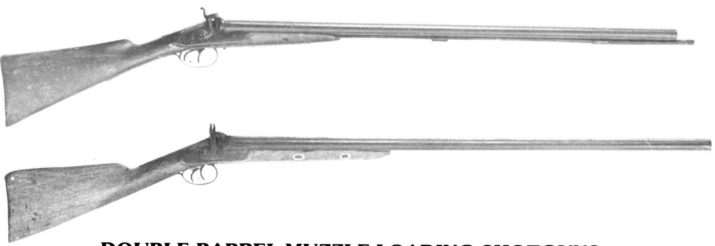

DOUBLE BARREL MUZZLE LOADING SHOTGUNS

The double barrel muzzle loader shown at the top of the photograph belonged to my grandfather, Rev. John G. Irwin, and presumably to his father, Edward Irwin.

The shotgun in the lower portion of the picture was acquired from my long-time friend, the late Guy Bowers of Greene County, Tennessee. Guy, who was one of the state's first collectors of "old timey things", said he wanted me to have his "Daddy's old gun". His father was Reuben Bowers, a Civil War veteran from Greene County. The Bowers family, of German descent, came from Pennsylvania into that rich, beautiful section of upper East Tennessee, along with many other German families in the late 1700's.

The lock on the Bowers gun is "Hollis and Sheath", and the inscription on the top is illegible. Guy recalls, as a lad, loading it too heavy and being kicked through a rail fence when he fired it.

WILEY GIBSON, GUNMAKER

The last of four generations of gunmakers, Wiley Gibson of the Walden's section of Sevier County, Tennessee (near Gatlinburg) is shown in these two photographs in his gun and blacksmith shop about 1937. (Photo by C.S. Grossman)

24

Lonnie Phillips is shown with his gun at the front of his home in the Cumberland Mountains

Although Lonnie Phillips has no furniture in his dirt-floored house which he built from sticks and small tree saplings, he does own a gun -- his most cherished possession. He is shown here in front of his house on a hot day in September 1978 in the Cumberland Mountains of Anderson County near Briceville, some fifteen miles west of the Museum.

Lonnie's home is miles from his nearest neighbor and can be reached only by a steep trail which winds around and over several ridges to the tiny huts where he lives -- moving at will from one to another. Although more of a hermit than most mountain men, Lonnie has retained the characteristic most common among the men of this region -- his love of guns.

When I asked Lonnie if he would go with me to another "house" he had built on the side of a distant mountain, he said, "Wait 'til I get my valuables." Whereupon he raked the leaves and sticks from an area near his house exposing a rectangular hole in the ground. From this he took a small burlap bag filled with some unknown items and the old shotgun which he had put together from parts of other guns he had found or otherwise acquired. Then he said, "All-right, now I'm ready to go." I don't think the gun would fire, and I'm quite certain that he had no shells for it; but he was brought up in a culture where the men would never think of strolling across mountains or meadow without a gun. (Photo by Steve Jernigan)

Alice Gibson was proud of her gun and her ability to use it

"I can shoot a gun and skin a varmint as good as any man ever you seen", declared Alice Gibson who lives in an area called Antioch Farm near the village of Norma in Scott County, Tennessee. "I catched and skinned this big 'possum last winter."

She proudly posed for this picture on her front porch step. Although hers is a modern shotgun, her love for hunting and for guns is a direct carryover from her mountain, frontier ancestors. When I asked if I could take her picture, she asked if I'd like to have her get her gun -- a most unusual suggestion for a woman about to pose for the camera.

"I never married -- jest stayed here in this old log house and took care of my Pap until he died -- and I learnt to hunt, fish, skin animals and sich as that from him." (Photo by the author, winter 1978)

26

S.L. Parker At Age 95

S.L. Parker of the Gibbs Community of neighboring Knox County loved and repaired guns for most of his long life. He is shown here, at age 95, outside his tiny shop holding an old pistol which he carried "off 'n on since I's a boy". Although a kind and gentle man, Parker emphasized that he "never wanted to be pushed around". The sign, which is partly visible, reads as follows: "Trading Post, Clocks, Gun Repairing". (Photo by Gordon Irwin about 1973)

MARION FISHER OF FISHERS BRANCH

On a recent visit with Marion we took some pictures of him feeding his hogs at his barn, and he asked if we'd like to get a picture of him with his guns. We assured him that we would and he had his daughter carry out a half dozen various types of pistols, rifles and shotguns from his modest little house. He was very proud of his guns and said, "I might just happen to have one stropped underneath my overalls right now."

He is shown here at age 82 demonstrating how he could still knock a squirrel from the distant white oak. His home is on Fishers Branch in Scott County, Virginia, some ten miles northeast of Kyles Ford, Tennessee. (Photo by Steve Jernigan)

CHAPTER II
THE SWAGE BLOCK OR GUN ANVIL

The oddly-shaped bulk of iron with its various-sized and shaped holes and indentations, when found lying in or nearby the closed down old blacksmith shops, is seldom recognized by the modern-day person. Never plentiful, at least in this region, it is not even familiar to most of the older folk.

When I first saw this tool many years ago, I was told that it was a dumb anvil, a term I have heard several times since. My friend and fellow collector, W.G. Lenoir, refers to it as a buffalo head, but I suppose the more correct name is a "Swage block." It, of course, is used to shape various-sized rods and bars by hands, as well as to make spoons and ladles in the round and oval depressed areas.

But if one of these odd relics turns up in a family where gunmaking was followed, it is a "gun anvil" and has been called that for several generations. One need not try to convince the party to the contrary. And, indeed, if the tool was used to forge the gun barrel, it would certainly be correct to refer to it as a gun anvil.

According to Eliot Wigginton, Wallace Gusler, the famous gunsmith at Williamsburg, could not find a single living soul who had first-hand knowledge of forging a gun barrel on the gun anvil. One reason for this is that many of the gunsmiths, even the old-timers, started buying factory-made barrels which they could rifle to their own notion. Gusler, after extensive research, came to the conclusion that a flat piece of metal was used for the barrel. It was heated repeatedly and literally wrapped around the rod or mandrel. But I have heard several claims by the mountain people that the gun barrels were made of various types of scrap metal, including horse shoes.

The gun anvil, or swage block, was obviously used for many purposes; and most of the rods and bars which could be made were considerably larger than a gun barrel. But it was, nevertheless, a most important tool for the gunmaker (possibly indispensable in making of a barrel) and merits inclusion in the study of the tools of the mountain gunmaker.

Once the barrel was forged on the gun anvil, it was usually ground to its traditional octagonal shape on a grindstone, often water powered. This would, of course, leave the bright, shiny raw steel surface which could not be tolerated. To remedy this, the exterior of the barrel had to be "blued". The following method was described in some detail by Hacker Martin in a letter to "The Muzzle-loader" in 1963, loaned to me by his daughter, Betty Martin Thompson.

Receipt For Browning Barrels By Hacker Martin

Leaving scientifick and learned discussions asside, it's very easy to BROWN iron - a handful of common salt in a gallon of rainwater will sorter do. Green walnut hulls are fairly good. So is hoss manure if old and well packed.

Many others will doubtless suggest themselves to the Gentle, Urbane and Reckless reader. In fact, about anything that will rust a barl will be all right. Main thing is not to leave the browner on too long like I do sometime and get the barl pitted-and have to refinish same-a sad task indeedy.

Here's how I go at it and it's about as satisfactory a way as you'll find. Stone or sand the iron bright and clean. If you get grease on it, you can rub some off very well with hard wood ashes in a minute or two. O.K.

I make the solution thusly: Use a quart of cheap alcohol, to keep her from freezing, and a quart of common cooking water. Rain or soft water is best, of course. Into that throw a handful of bluestone and an ounce or two of nitric acid. Fill up the gallon glass jug with chamber lye from your bed pot. Cork your jug and shake her up once in a while so the ingredients will dissolve and mix up good. Let set a week or two or use it at once as you see fit. It works all right at any age and while there's plenty more ways of making browner, I like this one very well; besides it beats paying $3.50 a pint for browner at ye dealers and likely works better and faster too. One ounce of corrosive sublimate of mercury will make it eat things up in short order, but it is not necessary.

I use it by smearing some on with a common cotton rag on a stick or with your fingers (NOT MINE) -- still I have never got burned with it in over 50 years. Let her rust overnight using a wire wheel or steel wool as you prefer. Smear on another coat and let rust again. So proceed until the brown looks about what you'd like it.

When you have good color, you can warm the barl and rub it with a piece of bees wax or other wax and a woolen rag. An old wool sock is all right.

If you want to be real fancy, you can varnish the work with clear, thin hard varnish -- one that dries fast is mighty good - most oldtimers used common shellack varnish, thinned very thin with alcohol, though some may prefer to drink the alcohol and use the shellack varnish as it is in the can.

If you do not have any chamber lye, I will be gald to furnish some for $2.00 per gallon. You come?

Steve Parkey sitting on the front porch of his Rebel Hollow home -- taken by the author a few weeks before Parkey's death.

→

← ## BILL PARKEY GUN ANVIL

This gun anvil came from old Bill Parkey's blacksmith shop which was located at the head of Rebel Hollow near the Powell River in Hancock County, Tennessee, and within a mile or so of Lee County, Virginia. I bought it from his son, the late Steve Parkey of the same area, pictured at left.

"That old 'dumb anvil' was made there at the head of Rebel Hollow," Steve told me. "They was an old iron foundry there way back in the old Rebel War."

The Parkeys, one of the very few Black families in that area, were master craftsmen. After Steve's death I bought out the entire blacksmith and wheelwright shop from the heirs. And there were many old gun parts, indicating that the family members were either makers or repairers of the old muzzle loaders.

The picture illustrates the manner by which the barrel was formed. The anvil formed half the circle. The concave hammer formed the other half into which the gun barrel was forged around a rod or mandrel, which was driven out when the barrel was completed.

29

Rowe Martin eighty-two-year old farmer, trader, bachelor and philosopher, sitting on his porch with the author in the cool of the evening. (Photo by Elizabeth Irwin)

ROWE MARTIN GUN ANVIL

This swage block is easily the most artistically-shaped one I have seen. Whether the scroll corners and the six pointed star were for aesthetic or utilitarian purposes is not known to this writer. The small grooves would have served the maker of a gun barrel well, and the even smaller grooves could have been used for making boring rods and rifling rods.

This gun anvil was bought, after much persuasion, from my old friend, Rowe Martin of near Limestone, birthplace of Davy Crockett. Rowe had acquired it from the old Jim Cochran blacksmith shop which was located in the village of Fall Branch, Tennessee, a few miles out of Jonesboro.

$\rightarrow$

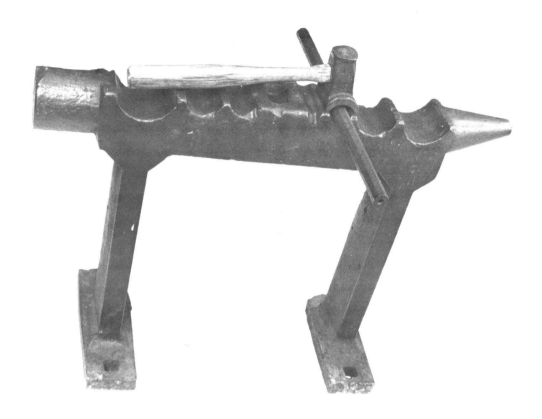

COMBINATION SWAGE BLOCK AND ANVIL
(Johnny Fincher Gun Anvil)

When Paul Wellborn, my trader friend from near Mosheim in Greene County, Tennessee, described this most unusual item he had found in an old blacksmith shop, I told him to buy it, if at all possible. He did buy it, but I was delayed for several weeks getting in touch with him, and the day I stopped by his place, he had sold it to our mutual friend Rowe Martin, mentioned earlier, and it was from Rowe that I finally acquired it. This is the first such item I have seen or even heard of, and none of my several expert acquaintances, nor any of my Museum visitors, were familiar with it.

One can forge different sizes of rods the same as on the conventional swage blocks, but this has the short horn which can be used to make horseshoes as one can do on the horn of an ordinary anvil. The horn has a small hole, the size of a 38 caliber bullet one inch from the end, for what purpose I don't know. It stands on legs about thirty inches high, and can be anchored by driving spikes through the four holes in the base. It obviously was made in a crude early mountain forge as it has many flaw cavities caused by impurities in the iron. Paul acquired it from the old Fincher place a few miles south of Greeneville in a community known as Hartman's Chapel.

Its last owner was "Uncle" Johnny Fincher, a farmer-blacksmith, who died about 1960 at the age of 87. This swage-anvil had belonged to Johnny's father, and earlier to his grandfather, according to the information given Paul. He also was told that the Finchers had at one time been gunmakers; so we may be correct in referring to the unusual item as a gun anvil.

DOW WEAVER GUN ANVIL

Like the Rowe Martin gun anvil, this one has small grooves which could be used for making rods for rifling, reaming, and "freshening" the rifle barrels. It was acquired from my longtime friend and collector of pioneer artifacts, Dow Weaver of Erie in Roane County, Tennessee. It is very crudely made, doubtless from one of the earliest forges in that area and is one of the smallest I have seen -- standing only nine inches in height. Close observation will reveal an indentation below the barrel which could be used for shaping a large spoon or a ladle.

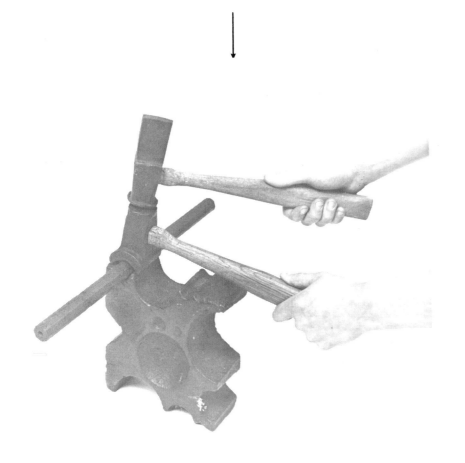

THE COX GUN ANVIL

The holes in this swage block allowed one to "true-up" the iron bars by driving them through the respective openings. The slight sway on the left side was probably designed to forge-weld wagon tires, and, of course, some of the half-rounds on top could have been used to forge the gun barrels. I purchased it from W.G. Lenoir who acquired it from the old Cox homeplace in the Hickory Valley section of Union County, Tennessee.

THE OLD TILSON WATER MILL

Shown here, in a picture taken about 1950, is Ben Tilson who has just received a "turn" of corn from Dave Farnor, a mill customer who lived on nearby Murray Branch. It was from the old Tilson Mill, located a few miles east of Erwin, Tennessee, that the Beals gun anvil remained after the gunshop was closed. (Photo courtesy of David Byrd)

WILLIAM BEALS' GUN ANVIL

According to David Byrd, the gun anvil pictured here belonged to William Beals, the gunmaker who made the rifle pictured on page 20. After the demise of the Beals gunshop, this relic came into the possession of the Tilson family, relatives of the Beals, and for many years sat at the Tilson's old watermill.

ERMON SLOAN AND HIS ANCESTRAL GUN ANVIL

Ermon Sloan lives a mile from where pioneer Archibald Sloan settled -- site of the early gunmaking shop discussed in Chapter III. He is a grandson of James Riley Sloan, Civil War veteran and resident of nearby Cagle Creek, and is a descendant of Squire Archibald Sloan.

This gun anvil belonged to his grandfather and, doubtless, came originally from the Sloan gunshop. I first "discovered" the treasured anvil about 1965, but Ermon elected not to part with it at that time. In the meantime, the Tennessee Valley Authority bought his homeplace for the Tellico Dam, and when I visited him recently, he said, "Well, me and my wife have been up to your Museum and I seen all your things, and I've about decided to let you have the old gun anvil for what you have offered. That way, you can sorta keep the old Sloan gun tools together, and the people can see 'em. It ain't doin' me no good layin' around here."

POTEET GUN ANVIL →

The crudest and possibly the oldest of the so-called gun anvils in the Museum, this one originated in Lee County, Virginia, near Jonesville from the old Poteet homeplace. This area was on one of the nation's best known early roads to the west (a few miles from Cumberland Gap) and was frequented by Dr. Thomas Walker, Daniel Boone and other early explorers. (Photo by the author)

CHAPTER III
THE SLOAN GUNBORING MACHINE

After the barrel was wrought and the rod removed from its bore, it was ready for boring, or, more properly, reaming. The hole, or bore, extending the length of the barrel would be quite irregular and would vary slightly in diameter after having been formed around the rod. Hence, the laborious task of "truing-up" was started. First, a square-ended rod would merely shave off the high points of the bore; then successively larger bits would be used -- perhaps as many as a dozen different sizes.

The gunboring "machine" at the Museum is the only old one I have found, or even heard about. It was the primary item from the old Sloan gunshop located in the Notchie section of Monroe County on the Tellico River and not far from the Great Smoky Mountains.

The large wheel was turned by a hand crank, driving a small pulley by means of a belt. Inserted in this pulley was the rod which was turned by the pulley. The rod extends into the muzzle of the gun barrel and is squared and tapered on this end. The rapidly revolving motion of the rod enlarges the bore of the barrel and shapes it to a uniform size. The weight attached to the carriage holding the barrel creates a constant pull of the carriage -- hence the carriage as well as the rifle barrel is constantly drawn into contact with the revolving rod.

I came upon the Sloan Family quite by accident. While driving on a back road in a community called Notchie, a few miles east of Madisonville, Tennessee, headed toward the Smoky Mountains in 1963, I stopped to give a ride to a stranger, Frank Sloan. After telling him of my interest in collecting mountain relics, he stated that his mother had some "old-timey things". He agreed to go with me and we found the exuberant old lady living in a mountain-type log house near the Tellico River. Her husband, John Sloan, had been dead for many years, and she was living with her daughter, Mrs. Catherine Patterson, and Mrs. Patterson's family in a quaint and picturesque setting.

Over the years I visited the family often and found them to be a most friendly and interesting people. In the summer, Mrs. Sloan always sat on the front porch of the log house a few feet from the hand-dug well which supplied water for the household. In the winter months, she, along with the other women, sat around the heating stove making quilts.

When I first knew the family, and for several years subsequent to my first visit, the Sloans were disturbed over the prospect that their ancestral home would be acquired by the Tennessee Valley Authority as a consequence of the building of the nationally controversial Tellico Dam. When it appeared that this project would become a reality, they began to sell many of the old frontier relics. And over a period of years I bought hundreds of artifacts from them, including the gunmaking equipment. They finally moved from the homeplace to a higher spot, overlooking the old log house which had served as a home for the Sloans since pioneer times. They waited a decade for the backwaters to come to cover their beloved ancestral home as the courts and Congress debated whether or not the nearly completed project should be pursued. The waters never came, but the weeds and groundhogs did, and the stately old home is falling into decay. In the meantime, the witty old lady of that homeplace, Mrs. Sloan, who was well into her nineties, died on the hill overlooking the old home.

Mrs. Sloan's husband, John Ross Sloan, who was several years her senior, had operated the gunshop from near the Civil War period. He had learned the trade and inherited the shop from his father, Madison Jackson Calloway Sloan, who presumably got it from his father. Archibald Sloan.

According to Mrs. Catherine Patterson, the great granddaughter of Archibald, he acquired the property as a land grant from the government in the early 1800's, and the property had never been sold until taken by the Tennessee Valley Authority. Many of the old papers of the Sloans, some dating to 1821, are in possession of the Pattersons.

Archibald Sloan was a Justice of the Peace, or Squire, and in that capacity had broad legislative and judicial powers in local matters. Tradition has it that he was Irish and that he, perhaps, had come directly from Ireland to this most remote wilderness region.

THE SLOAN GUNBORING MACHINE

Roy Sherwood, an employee of the Museum of Appalachia, is shown here at the gunmaking display, demonstrating the gunboring machine.

The barrel is wedged into its position in the carriage of the gunboring machine. As the revolving bit works its way into the barrel, the taut string pulls the carriage and the barrel into the rotating path of the reaming rod. →

Mrs. John Sloan is shown here in 1968 with a cousin, Paul Cagle, sitting on the porch of the ancestral log house built by gunmaker and pioneer Archibald Sloan. (Photo by the author about 1964)

↓

Frank Sloan, great, great grandson of gunmaker Archibald Sloan who is believed to have fashioned the gunboring machine in the early 1800's, is shown here at his home, in Monroe County, Tennessee, a few miles east of Madisonville, home of the late Senator Estes Kefauver. (Photo by the author)

CHAPTER IV
THE RIFLING GUIDE AND ACCESSORIES

It has often occurred to me that the simple device used for cutting the tiny grooves, or rifles, inside the gun barrel actually altered the course of American history. The old smooth-bore musket was so inaccurate that a would-be pioneer could have no assurance that he could kill enough game to sustain himself in the wilderness until his first crop was harvested. And for whatever reasons, the Indians often presented an awesome threat to life and family as well as to livestock and property, making the rifle a "life or death" possession.

There is no doubt that the rifled gun encouraged the settlement of what was then known as the West, because one could feel relatively safe with this remarkably accurate weapon -- the Kentucky rifle. A good marksman could bring down a deer at a distance which would have been practically impossible with a "non-rifled" gun.

How did man hit upon the idea that a series of spiraled grooves cut inside the bore of the rifle would so greatly improve its accuracy? And how, even more baffling, did he devise a means of cutting these rifles at precise intervals, without the benefit of precision tools?

Research indicates that the first experiments with rifling guns were conducted by the Germans. The Smithsonian owns what is considered to be the earliest rifle, a German piece, made in the late 1400's for Maximilian I, ruler of the Holy Roman Empire.

It shall not be our purpose here to speculate on how the rifling process was conducted in Europe, or even in Pennsylvania where it was perfected. Rather we shall look at how it was done in the early wilderness area of Southern Appalachia where sophisticated tools and specialized trades were even more scarce than in Europe three hundred years earlier.

Charlie Blevins is the only man I know who ever rifled guns the old-fashion way. Charlie lives in a community called "Sheep Range" in Fentress County, Tennessee, about half way between the world-famous Sgt. Alvin C. York's home and the home of U.S. Sen. Howard Baker. His little mountain homestead can be reached by traveling several miles through the woods, and his is the last house on the road. "When ye git to my place, you're at the end of the road", he laughed. And then he added: 'Whenever I see

a car comin', I know they're either coming to see me or they're lost, one or 'tuther."

Not only has he rifled the barrels, he has made three of the rifle guides (in the early part of the century), and at a time when this tool was already an obsolete relic in other parts of the country. (Two of the guides are now part of the permanent gun display at the Museum.)

Charlie explained to Eliot Wigginton and me how he made and used his rifling "machine". "Well I learn't the trick of makin' the rifle guide from my Daddy, and I reckon he learn't it from his Daddy. He lived way up near the Kentucky line at a place called 'Parched Corn'.

"First", Charlie explained, "I took a pole -- I made mine out of poplar -- 58 inches long and 3½ inches in diameter. The pole has to be jest about perfectly round, no humps nor flat places."

Charlie went on to point out that he uses five grooves in his rifling guide. By means of a chalk line, Charlie would mark the path the groove was to be cut in the cylindrical pole. It would make one revolution in 58 inches. After the five grooves were marked, Charlie went to work to cut the grooves, about ⅜ of an inch deep. This he did with a pocket knife and one or two simple chisels.

On one end of this grooved guide he attaches a revolving type handle, and into the other end he attaches a rod the same length as the grooved guide. A piece of metal with tiny saw teeth was inserted into the center of this rod, but near the end opposite the one attached to the guide. The guide is then mounted on a table and the spiral grooves pass through a circular notched wooden block. As the guide is pushed forward it turns slowly, as does the rod attached to the guide. The saw-cutter thus cuts a small grove inside the rifle barrel which is attached to the opposite end of the bench and into which the rod is forced.

When the groove, or rifle, is cut the first time, the guide is taken out of its wooden notched block and moved one notch, having the effect of scoring another groove inside the barrel a fraction of an inch from the first and precisely following the degree of "twist" of the first groove. This process is repeated until all five grooves have been cut. Then the saw is removed from the rod and "shimmed up" with a thin piece of paper so as to allow the saw, or cutter, to protrude a bit more and thus to cut a bit deeper groove as it is forced in and out of the rifle barrel. After the second cutting, the cutter is removed and shimmed again; and so on until the rifles have been cut as deeply as one desires. He uses hog grease as a lubricant for the cutter.

Charlie has always declared that it takes one long hard day to rifle a gun barrel "if everything goes right". He does not always use the same twist, but varies the degree of the spiral depending upon "how a man aimed to load his rifle". He believes that a light ball and a heavy charge of powder require less twist in the rifles than a heavy ball with a light charge for accuracy.

Some gunmakers would increase the rate of the twist of the rifle toward the muzzle of the barrel. This presumably had the effect of increasing the spinning motion of the bullet at an increasing rate as it traveled through the barrel; and ostensibly further increasing the accuracy of the path of the projectile. But Charlie did not attempt any of these more sophisicated rifling techniques.

Although Hacker Martin worked in this century, his techniques, as noted earlier, represented the style used by the pioneer gunsmith. For that reason we are including, in his own words, Hacker's description of the rifling process as he wrote it for "The Muzzleloader" in 1963.

How We Hand-Rifle Them in Tennessee and Virginia by Hacker Martin

Due to numerous letter inquiring as to how we manage to rifle a 48" barrell in about one hour using a sub-teenager for power; I will proceed to explain the method or system we now use.

First. The saw is the heart of the matter. It is made with the teeth rounding from end to end, the end teeth about 1/16" shorter than the middle teeth, 6 or 7 teeth are about right. I often make the saws from high speed special steel, old dull power hacksaw blades are all right. Break and grind them to shape with teeth ground to a skew if you want them so. Saws to be about 2/3 of the bore diameter and length about 3 times the same, say ¾" or ⅞". Note this: The teeth are made with a back rake, the reverse of a hook, that's a few degrees blunt, but have them keen enough to catch on a finger nail easily or else it will take too long to rifle the barl. Sharpness is what we must have if we are to get along fast and slick. We use a plain hickory ramrod head about 5 or 6 inches long, set into the rifling rod. Blunt all edges that fit into the wood or soon you will have a loose saw. If you fear the saw may work loose end-wise, drill a ⅛" hole through the wood at each end of the saw and set in brass pins tightly, or if you want to be scientific, you can run a ring of babbit around each end of the saw in a groove cut around the wood and a groove from them to the end of the wooden head. Heat the barl til it frys spit before running in the babbit if you expect a good cast. I never use this as I deem it unnecessary. And, be sure the saw, head, etc., will push through the bore with much ease the FIRST time, or else you might get a stuck saw.

With a free-running worm we are ready to do the dirty work. So, grease the rifling head with sperm whale oil if you have some, if not bears oil or if not that use common hog lard which is about as good as anything and cheap, run through the barl once to be sure all is easy. Back out. Raise up the saw, slip a paper shim under, mash the saw down with brass jawed pliers tightly. Try again until you are scraping of a slight swarf of dirt (steel iron). Work until you are not doing much good. Shim her up again and so proceed until you get the grooves as deep as you think good. I consider that .006 - .008" is plenty. I use Robert Chadwick barls as they are tough, straight, smooth, and cut as easy as you can want. I have found no better barrel blanks.

As to how often to wipe off the swarf or chips from the rifler, I often rifle the whole job without wiping out the barl. Simply take an old tooth brush and wipe off any outside chips and shavings. The sperm oil or lard will bring out about all cuttings with it, so why worry? If any chips get back of the saw on the wooden rifling head, they will bed into it and serve to polish the tops of the lands, and all scratches (if any) being parallel to the rifling they will cause no trouble from wild shooting, quite the contary.

A carbon steel saw properly tempered will need touching up with a hard stone a few times for each barl. Harden them in warm water and draw to a dark straw or even a brown color. You can temper them so you can sharpen them with a file and they will still cut as much and as long as when left harder. A very hard saw will tend to crumble which is the worse state ever.

Temper to a dark barley straw color will likely hold on edge the longest. Never overheat your steel. A good bright red in the dark is about right for forging and hardening most carbon steels. By having your saw rounded on top, the two middle teeth will cut good. When they wear down a mite, the next teeth on each end will take hold. Always sharpen only the dull teeth.

Always ream the ends of your barl about 1/16" beveled. This is to prevent your saw from catching on the edges of the bore; a calamity to be avoided by all means. Never fool with a dull saw nor try to cut after the saw has gotten easy to pull through as that will work harden the bottoms of the grooves. Keep the saw cutting at all times. Don't forget the grease.

Your worm must work easy. A loose worm will not mess up the rifling unless it's over 1/8" wobbling sidewise; or more. I get about 3 barls rifled with one sharpening of a power hacksaw blade. But, be sure to touch them up when you notice the least dullness.

That's about it, as I believe. Write to the good old "Muzzleloader" if you want more advice on this or any other rifle subject. Do not write to me as I have to WORK for a living and not much of a living at that. Note-in making a rifling worm of wood you saw out the first one with saw and chisel, etc. Use this one as a guide to plane out the others by; set up a wooden finger and a chisel clamped in to cut all other grooves.

Once the rifling process was completed, one end of the barrell was sealed off by means of an iron breech plug, and a touch hole bored into the side of the barrel a half-inch from the end. It was through this tiny hole that the spark of fire from a percussion cap, or from flint, would ignite the powder, create the explosion inside the barrel and force the bullet through and out the bore. Should the explosion, or firing of the rifle, cause a crack or break in the breach end of the barrel, it could be most dangerous to the person firing it because his face, for the purpose of sighting, would be positioned within a few inches of the area most likely to erupt. To make sure the new barrel was safe, it was customary to load it heavy -- often with four times the usual amount of powder, and to fire it from a distance by means of a string attached to the trigger. If it withstood the test, then it was reasonable to assume that it would be safe under normal conditions and for a prolonged period.

CHARLIE BLEVINS "FAST" TWIST RIFLE GUIDE

This photograph shows the rifling guide pushed forward almost to its limit. The cutting rod has thus been extended almost the entire length of the rifle bore. Note the rapid spiral or twist on this guide compared to the one shown on the opposite page. This guide was also made by Charlie Blevins of Fentress County, Tennessee. The rifle barrel resting on the bench came from the famous gunmaker, Hacker Martin.

THE CHARLIE BLEVINS RIFLE GUIDE

Here the guide is pushed forward, turning the attached rod and cutting the groove or rifle inside the barrel by means of a small cutter inserted into the side of the rod. Note the slow twist on this guide made by Charlie Blevins -- consisting of only one revolution in 58 inches.

MARY OWENBY MAKING A RIFLE GUIDE

Matt Owenby and his wife Mary were among those mountain folk who continued to make the muzzle loading rifle into the 20th century. They lived in the Glades Community of Sevier County just north of Gatlinburg. Here Mary is shown, first turning a true cylindrical wooden rod on the ancient spring pole turn lathe. (The spring pole, itself, is barely visible in the shaded portion of the shed.)

In the second photograph she is shown using a wooden splint to mark the degree of the rifles to be cut. And in the third picture she is shown with the nearly completed rifle guide. The guide consists of seven grooves, each making one complete twist in the 48-inch length of the guide. Matt Owenby is discussed with illustrations in Chapter V in connection with gunmaking tools. (Photos courtesy of Ed Trout and the Great Smoky Mountain National Park)

MATT OWENBY "DRESSING OUT"
A NEWLY RIFLED BARREL

Matt Owenby is shown here in the mid 1930's dressing out a barrel he has recently rifled. The hickory dressing rod had a lead plug on the end, molded in the barrel, thereby having the imprint of the rifles to expedite the process. (Photo courtesy of Ed Trout and the Great Smoky Mountain National Park)

Here Charlie explains to Eliot Wigginton and me how the rifle guide is turned as it is pushed into the wood block which has teeth which correspond and fit into the grooves in the guide. The barrel would be wedged in the holes in the two blocks at far left. (Photo by Eliot Wigginton.)

Charlie Blevins explains how he carved the grooves in this rifling guide. Note the cutting rod inserted into the end of the guide, which turns in direct and precise relation to the guide. (Photo by Eliot Wigginton)

Old time gunmaker Will Howell (1877-1959) of Flat Top Mountain, North Carolina, whose rifle guide is shown on the top of the page, and whose gunmaking tools are discussed in Chapter IV, is shown here holding one of his recently completed rifles. (Photo courtesy of Mrs. Pete Howell)

WILL HOWELL'S RIFLE GUIDE

Apparently Will Howell did not have a conventional rifle guide, thus he improvised one of his own, which did not require the grooved spiral guide at all. It worked as follows: a barrel, which had previously been rifled was secured on a bench to the right; then a rod was inserted into the rifled barrel. The end of this rod has a molded lead impression of the rifles inside the barrel, so as to cause the lands and ridges to fit snugly into the barrel. And as the rod was removed from the rifle barrel, it turns in direct relation to the rifles. On the opposite end of the rod is the saw-type cutter which is pulled into the unrifled barrel as it is removed from the other, thus cutting rifles inside the new barrel precisely as they existed in the old one.

This device, of course, could only be used to duplicate the same twist as the "guide" barrel; and it was only useful if one had a barrel already rifled. In other words, it could not take the place of the primary rifle guide. Additionally, it was a much slower process than when using the more conventional method. Will's son, Pete Howell, recalls that it took his father about 24 hours to rifle a single barrel using his system.

All the gunmaking tools made and used by Howell are pictured and described in Chapter V, along with additional information on the Howell gunmaking family of Flat Top Mountain, North Carolina.

Boy Snodderly, who lived at the old homeplace, is shown here about 1934 with a rifle made by his grandfather, Henry Snodderly. (Photo by Marshall Wilson)

The rifle guide shown here was made and used by Henry Snodderly. Note the two metal steeples at right into which the barrel was placed and wedged. (Photo by Marshall Wilson)

THE HENRY SNODDERLY HOMEPLACE

Henry Snodderly had come from North Carolina in pioneer times as a twenty-one year old man and settled on Hinds Creek where he operated a water-powered grist mill, farmed, and made rifles. The Snodderlys and the Rices intermarried and George Rice at one time had as his partner, George Snodderly, his brother-in-law. Henry Snodderly was a first cousin to George Rice.

Old Henry was murdered, along with his wife, as they sat before the fire on the night of February 8, 1894. Henry was 90 years of age and his wife, Serena, 75. Their murderers, Clarence Cox and John Stanley, were later captured and hanged in the nearby town in Maynardville.

My grandfather, Sill Rice, was a witness to the hanging and vividly recalled that the older Stanley pleaded that the life of his young companion, sixteen year old Cox, be spared. But the sheriff had his orders and the teenager was soon dangling from the scaffold with his older partner in crime, and his father was there to claim the body. (Photo by Marshall Wilson)

RICE GUNS AND RIFLING GUIDE

Shown here are the two rifles made by my great, great grandfather George Rice, along with the rifling rods at left, and the rifle guide at right. The hunting pouch and powder horn are shown hanging in the doorway. The photograph was taken about 1934 by Marshall Wilson at the old Rice homeplace in Big Valley in adjoining Union County, and prior to the time when the inhabitants were forced out of their ancestral homes by the Tennessee Valley Authority for the building of Norris Dam, the first in a series of many.

SMOKY MOUNTAIN RIFLE GUIDES

The small rifle guide shown here, in the top of the photograph, was from the gunmaking shop of Tim Quilliam in Sevier County, Tennessee, and the larger one belonged to gunmaker George Kellog whose shop was near the village of Parrotsville in Cocke County, Tennessee. (Photograph taken Circa 1937 by H.C. Wilburn)

50

CHAPTER V
TOOLS OF THE MOUNTAIN GUNMAKER

In thinking back over my years of collecting thousands of gunmaking tools in this southern mountain region, it occurred to me that I found none that were factory-made -- they all were made by the gunsmith who used them. A classic example of the ingenuity of the mountain gunsmith making all his tools from scrap pieces of iron and steel, is that of William Howell of Flat Top Mountain in Yancy County, North Carolina, discussed earlier in connection with his improvised rifle guide.

I visited the old Will Howell homeplace and talked with his aging son, Pete, and with Pete's wife who remembered vividly the details of Will Howell's gunmaking. Pete was not feeling well and she did most of the talking.

It was a cool October day and the modest little house looked even smaller because of the mountains which towered over it. The tiny blacksmith shop, which was also the gun shop, had washed away in a flood some two years previously.

"Now Will Howell, that's Pete's daddy, could make anything", Mrs. Howell stated.

"He'd make them gun barrels out of wagon tires -- he'd cup them up and around a rod. Of course, he had to keep them red hot when he's aworkin' with them. Then, after he made the barrel, he'd drive the rod out.

"If a body came by and wanted a hog rifle, he'd light in and make it from scratch. He could make one in a week and a half, but he was very particular. I've set and watched him whittle out the thinnest little shavin' ever you seed, then he'd put the stock down in that groove, and if it didn't fit perfectly, he'd take it out and shave off a little more. Lord, he had patience."

"He'd done most of the stock work with a pocket knife, and the iron work with a hammer. He'd need a piece for the gun, a lock or a spring, and he'd go down to the shop and build him up a fire, and in a little while he'd come back with it all finished."

"He'd git $35 to $40 for a gun", Mrs. Howell continued. "And he done an awful lot of blacksmith work fer the loggers and farmers. He always kept busy."

I asked her where he learned the art of gunmaking. "Why, from his Daddy -- his name was Pete too, same as his boy, my man. Old Pete died in 1925, and he'd made hog rifles all his life."

In response to a question about where the Howells originated, she said, "Why I allus heard that they's Airish (Irish)."

Will's son, Pete, took up gunmaking in a limited way, but never rivaled his father nor his grandfather in quantity, and probably not in quality.

"My Pete here made 52 cap 'n ball pistols, and we don't have airy one left. And he never made but one rifle gun, and we don't even hav it. I oughten to say it, but he wasn't as good as his Daddy when hit come to makin' guns."

Will Howell and his wife, Ida Bell, are shown on the steps of their Yancy County, North Carolina home in this picture taken in the 1940's. (Photo courtesy of Mrs. Pete Howell)

THE WILL HOWELL GUNSHOP ⟶

This is the only picture of the little gun and blacksmith shop where three generations of gunsmiths produced many beautiful Kentucky rifles. It was destroyed by a flood in 1977. Family members in the foreground are: front row, Mrs. Cindy Hensley and Richard Hensley, parents of Mrs. Pete Howell; sitting at right is Pete and in the back is Usely Booker and Neoma Watts.

52

Pete Howell of Flat Top Mountain is shown with the only rifle he ever made, though he made 52 cap and ball pistols. (Photo taken in 1952 by Mrs. Howell)

Pete Howell, old and enfeebled, enjoys a patch of sunlight on a chilly October (1979) morning on the front porch of his home on Flat Top Mountain, North Carolina. Shuck beans, or leather britches, are hung to dry (shown in the top of the photo) and turnips, recently pulled from the garden, are shown at right. But the plastic flower pots, clorox bottles, and metal chairs betray the fact that "civilization" has come to the mountains. (Photo by the author)

← This walnut pistol stock, never finished, was found in the woodshed at Pete Howell's home. (Photo by the author).

WILL HOWELL'S BOW DRILL

Although this simple but effective tool was developed by various stone age civilizations, it was reemployed in Appalachia and was used even into the Twentieth Century here. Of the very few I have found, over half are known to have come from small mountain gunmakers. The drill is shown here being used to bore a small hole into the rifle lock plate.

The firedrill, which is identical in principle to the bow drill, was known to have been used at least 3,000 years ago, as the drill sockets, the stationary handhold, have been found and dated to that period. Examples of this type tool, dating back to 800 B.C., have been reported in Egypt; and Homer in the **Odyssey** describes the strap drill (which is very similar to the bow drill) in his work about 900 B.C. The Eskimo had developed the bow drill, (as had the North American Indians) with which they produced beads and other ornamental items.

According to my friend, Percy W. Blandford, the English writer and authority on early tools, this device did not survive in Britain. Presumably it was abandoned for more sophisticated drills and augers.

HOWELL'S GUNMAKING DRILL AND BITS

Shown here with the bow drill are six extra bits of varying sizes and shapes which could be interchanged with the one presently in the shaft.

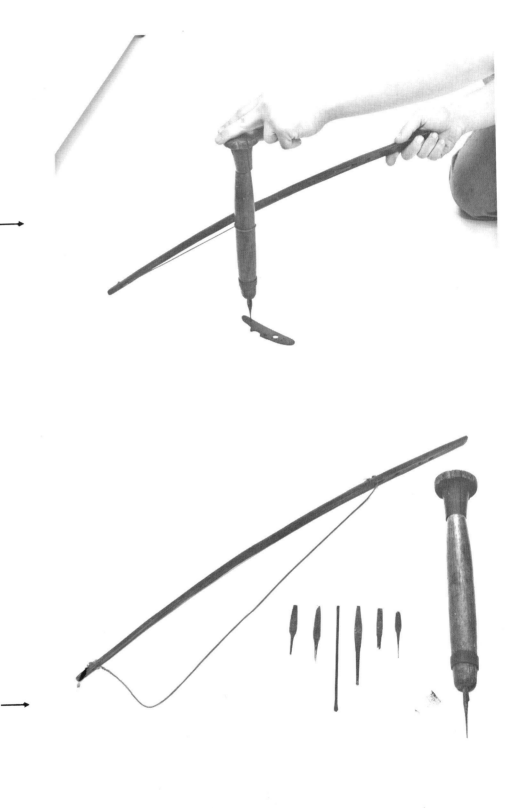

When Will Howell needed screws, bolts or taps for his guns, he made them. But special tools were needed and he made from scrap metal the tools needed to make other tools such as taps and dies for cutting the inside and outside threads, shown in this photograph.

Various sized and shaped chisels and punches were made by Howell for cutting metal and for punching holes. All were made from worn-out rasps, files and other discarded metal.

WILL HOWELL'S TOOLS FOR MAKING GUN STOCKS

These four small wooden planes and the seven chisels were made by Howell for shaping and finishing his graceful gunstocks. Here again, most all the metal parts were made from abandoned files and rasps.

HOWELL'S INSCRIBING TOOLS

The only tool of this sort I have seen, it was inserted into the chuck of a brace and used to cut a circular groove in the end of the barrel. An adjustment on the cutter allowed one to make a series of circles from near the bore to the outer portion of the barrel. This was apparently for decorative purposes only, but may have served to identify Howell's guns as well -- a sort of trademark.

WILL HOWELL'S CHERRIES

These five bullet mold cherries were made by Howell to cut the cavity inside the bullet mold -- different sized cutters created various sized molds. The manner in which the tools were made is illustrated on page 100.

For years I had wanted some handmade tool or artifact from the gunshop of the nationally-renowned Hacker Martin who lived and worked in an old wooden-geared gristmill on Cedar Creek in Washington County in upper East Tennessee. (Hacker's illustrious career was discussed in Chapter I in connection with his flintlock pistol which is on display at the Museum.)

My acquisition of some of Hacker's tools came about in a round-about way. My friend, Eliot Wigginton, the man who founded the Foxfire Project in Rabun Gap, Georgia (and in doing so influenced the direction of formal education more than any man in America during recent years), was working on his fifth Foxfire book, much of which was to be devoted to guns and gunmaking in the Southern Appalachian region. And, naturally, he spent considerable time and research on Hacker Martin, interviewing scores of people including Betty Jean, Hacker's daughter. In reminiscing about what had happened to the many great pieces Hacker made, Eliot told her of the flintlock pistol which I had displayed in the Museum of Appalachia.

It was two years before Betty came by the Museum. I was working with the men, cutting timbers to be used for mounting an old tan bark mill, when a lady approached me and said, "I'm Hacker Martin's daughter, and I just wanted to tell you what a wonderful job you've done here in preserving our heritage."

She and her husband, Charles Thompson, still lived at the old homeplace on Cedar Creek and owned the grist mill and gunshop building where Hacker had worked. When I told them of my interest in acquiring some of Hacker's relics, they stated that theives had carried off some of the artifacts, and others had been sold, but that I was welcome to come and see what might be left.

Within a few days I went with my friend Elmo Johnson, an official with the Tennessee Department of Education, to Greene County looking for relics from that historic area. It was a windy day in late November (1979) and at 4 o'clock we were cold, hungry, and had not bought one article. Since we were within a few miles of the Hacker Martin Mill, we decided to go by, although I was not at all excited about the prospects -- realizing that antique dealers, as well as pillagers, had frequented the place.

It was almost dark when we arrived, and getting colder; and we were invited into the kitchen by Betty for tea; then to the buildings I had heard so much about: the water-powered corn mill, and the Hacker Martin gunshop and living quarters building.

Charles allowed us to go through the entire three floors of both buildings, searching through the shelves, boxes, and workbenches for any of Hacker's tools and, to my amazement, we found dozens of the old gunmaking tools. After a brief horse-trading session with Charlie and after consulting Betty on the painting and a few other items, I was able to purchase the relics; and back to the warm kitchen for more tea and a wee bit of Betty's homemade wine.

These tools of the trade, shown on the following pages, were virtually all made by Hacker and give insight into the ingenious nature of this legendary gunsmith. They are now on display at the Museum, along with the tools and relics from scores of other gunsmiths of the region.

Shown here are two close-up views of the flintlock, every piece of which was made by Hacker in the 1920's. The masonry building at right was built beside the old mill after he outgrew the gunmaking room in the mill. (Photo by the author)

Betty Jean Martin Thompson, only daughter of Hacker, is shown here with her husband Charles in front of the old wooden-geared grist mill on Cedar Creek which Hacker operated, and which once served as his gunmaking shop. Charles is holding one of the guns Hacker made. (Photo by the author.)

This view of Hacker's water-powered grist mill, right, and the gunshop was painted by the father of Jesse Patterson, a "boy who used to work for Daddy," according to Betty. It was acquired from the Thompsons along with the other items from the mill and gunshop. The elder Patterson, a disabled veteran who lived in nearby Johnson City, never visited the mill and gunshop and is said to have painted the realistic picture based on his son's description of it. (Photo by Ed Meyer)

→

←

Among the items found in the gunshop was this crude engraving in steel of the water mill which Hacker operated after he left Tennessee and moved to Appomattox, Virginia. Since it was engraved in reverse fashion, it apparently was intended for printing. (Photo by Ed Meyer)

STONE BULLET MOLD

This early bullet mold, carved from stone, was among the relics Hacker traded for in his gunmaking days. It is believed by some to have been made by the Indians during the years they used firearms which they had acquired from the White traders; others believe that the mold was made by the early Whites. It is decorated on the entire outer surface with half-circle designs and produces a bullet of about 50 caliber in size. (Photo by Ed Meyer)

STONE PIPE

This Indian pipe made from stone was another of Hacker's trade items acquired by the Museum. The crudely carved wild turkey decorates the bowl. (Photo by the author)

GUNSTOCK ROUTING TOOL

This most unusual tool, a type of drawing knife, was apparently made by Hacker to cut the grooves in the stock in which the rifle barrel rested. (Photo by Ed Meyer)

HACKER MARTIN'S GUNSTOCK TOOLS

Scattered throughout the dirt-floored shop, we found these tools which Hacker had used to carve his graceful stocks. All these woodworking tools were handmade, presumably by him, except the dual purpose plane shown at the lower right. (Photo by the author)

DRAWING KNIVES

These drawing knives were likely used in the early stages of making the stock. (Photo by the author)

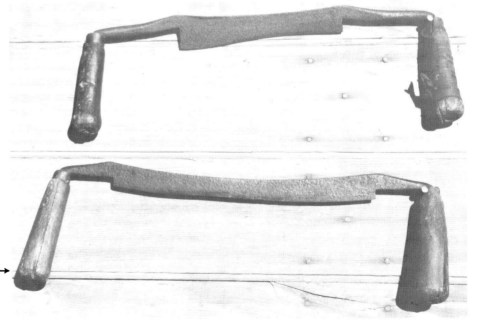

GUNSTOCK CARVING TOOLS

This assortment of tools which Hacker had made for carving various sections of the rifle stocks were found in a bucket half-full of oil where they had been carefully placed to protect them from rust. Most of them are made from old rasps and files which make an excellent tool if tempered by an expert blacksmith such as Hacker. (Photo by the author)

SCREW PLATE

It has been said that Hacker made every piece which went into his early rifles, including the screws, and this die for cutting the threads adds credence to that claim. (Photo by the author)

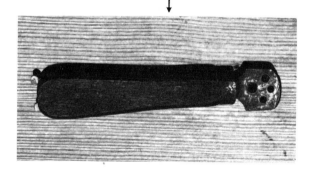

The wooden mallet, left, was used to drive the chisel for mortising the stock for the lock, the trigger mechanism, etc. At right is a small bullet-shaped hammer which may have been used to shape various brass accouterments on the gun. (Photo by the author)

HANDFORGED GUN BARREL

Hacker Martin is believed to have been one of the very last gunsmiths in America to have made the gun barrel by hand. This one is so well made by him that it requires close inspection to detect that it is handforged. The tongs are designed especially for holding the gun barrel, and the swage hammer was used in the forging process.

HACKER'S BLACKSMITH TONGS

In addition to being an expert woodworker, a gunsmith had to be a master blacksmith. These four tongs were made by Hacker to suit his specific needs. The tool shown in the upper right was used to keep the air hole in the fire open, and to feed coal to the fire in just the needed amounts. (Photo by the author)

This is a device whose purpose is not known to the writer. It works much like a type of pencil sharpener but would cut a much more gradual taper -- no sharp end could be produced. When found in Hacker's shop, it had the wooden peg with the cross handle inserted in the hole; so it was assumed that the two pieces were used in concert.

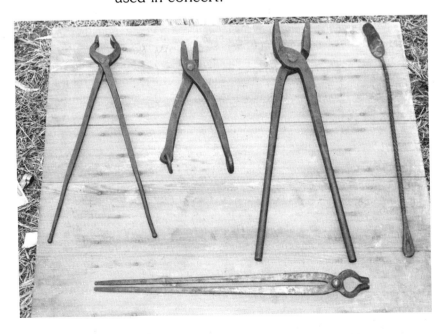

64

The purpose of this tool, shown in its open and closed position, is not known to the writer. It appears to be a mold for making tapered lead rods, but this is conjecture.

FLINTLOCK

Although this crudely-forged flintlock was found in Hacker's shop, it is unlikely that he ever had any intentions of using it on one of his rifles. It is larger than the locks he used, and its rough character would not have been consistent with Hacker's fine rifles. Some students of the Kentucky rifle would date this lock to the early 1700's. (Photo by the author)

SIGHT MOLDS

As one may surmise, Hacker Martin was an ingenious man, and several unusual, or even unique, tools were found in his abandoned shop. The item shown here appears to be a pair of molds for forming the rifle sights which were to be mounted on the barrel. →

Although peep sights were not used, to my knowledge, on the Kentucky rifles, Hacker made this one from lead, perhaps for testing purposes.

TALLOW TEMPERING BOXES

The trigger mechanism of a good rifle required the precision of a fine clock, and the gunsprings especially had to be tempered properly. The rapidity at which a piece of metal is allowed to cool, of course, determines its hardness and resiliency. Most blacksmiths used water, but there were other ways to cool the metal and the Sloans used these dug-out poplar boxes filled with sheep's tallow. Some of the dried tallow still remains in the bottom of the trough.

BULLET MOLDS

The brass bullet mold at right was apparently made by Hacker since it bears his signature; the other tool appears to be a double mold, except the back portion is open and could only be used to mold bullets if it were set in sand while in use. Again, a product of Hacker's design and perhaps only he knew its purpose. (Photo by the author)

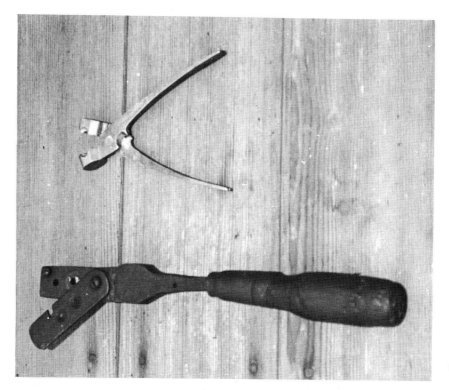

SLOAN GUN VICE →

Several years after I had bought the old Sloan gunshop, discussed earlier, I was visiting Frank Sloan, son of John, the last gunmaker to use the shop. In going through some old boxes stored in the loft of one of his little buildings, I found this crudely handmade vice. Frank was delighted: "I've been a'wonderin' fer years what ever became of Grandpap's old gun vice. I had looked and looked fer it -- finally figured somebody had stole it -- now ain't that somethin'?"

At first, Frank wanted to keep it but decided it would be better to sell it to me "so more people can see it and see how the old people had to make everything from scratch."

The small lockplate in the jaws of the vice illustrates how small the vice is. Its shape and construction, however, are very similar to the large blacksmith shop vices which are a hundred times larger.

← PARKEY GUN VICE

This very small double-adjustment type vice was bought from the gun, blacksmith, and wheelwright shop of the Parkeys of Rebel Hollow, Hancock County, Tennessee (the Parkey shop was discussed more fully earlier in connection with the swage block). Steve Parkey, from whom I purchased the vice, stated that it was made by his father, Bill Parkey, and that it was used "for working on guns." The entire length of the jaws is only eight inches.

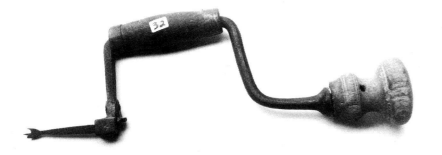

WOODEN BRACE

This very early handmade brace is more crudely made than those made in Sheffield, England, during the 1700's. I purchased this one from Paul Ryan of Falls Branch, located between Kingsport, Jonesboro, and Greeneville, Tennessee. He acquired it from that area. A brace such as this was used by the gunsmith for cutting a seat for the lock in the stock, for boring the tallow hole, etc.

FRESHENING ROD

These lead rods were molded inside the rifle to be freshened. A cutter was attached to the end of the rod for deepening the rifles and the molded lead portion of the rod served as a guide, following the old grooves or rifles inside the barrel. These came from the Sloan gunshop, previously discussed. (Photo by the author)

STOCK RABBETING TOOL

Made from a worn-out file, this is a most effective tool to cut the rabbet or channeled groove into which the barrel rested. I acquired it from Fred Carter of Clintwood, Virginia, who indicated it came from an old gunmaker of that area by the name of Honaker.

69

CHARLIE BLEVINS
AND HIS BOW DRILL

Charlie is shown here using the bow drill he made and used in his gunmaking shop. A close-up photograph of the same drill is shown at right. The handle, or drill socket, remains stationary, while the shaft rotates in a "back and forth" fashion. (Charlie and his gunmaking are discussed earlier as is the history of the bow drill.)

WILEY GIBSON
WITH HIS BOW DRILL

The last of four generations of gunmakers, Wiley Gibson is shown here using the ancient bow drill in his shop at Waldens in Sevier County, Tennessee. This photograph was taken in the mid 1930's by C.S. Grossman.

TRIP HAMMER

This trip hammer, or helve hammer, weighing about 400 pounds was used by pioneer gunmaker James Rice to process iron and steel needed for his rifles and for other purposes. It was attached to one end of a lever and was lifted by the water-powered millwheel. The hammer was tripped automatically and fell of its own weight striking the iron being processed. This historic, pioneer relic remained with the old wooden-geared mill from the time it was built in the 1790's until it was given to the Smithsonian Institution a few years ago. (Photo by Melvin Little)

BLEVINS GUNSTOCK PLANES

These two crude and simple planes were made by Charlie to make his walnut gunstocks. While some "up east" gunmakers may have used dozens of finely made hand planes and woodworking tools for making gunstocks, Charlie used only these two. The top one is a general purpose type and the one shown at the bottom of the photograph was used to cut the groove into which the barrel was fitted.

THE PUMP DRILL

The pump drill, or pump auger, also dates to antiquity, with some of the early ones having shell or stone for the cutter or bit. The earliest mention of the pump auger I know of was by Theophilus about 1100 A.D., but it was apparently invented independently by primitive races throughout the world. As the name implies, the drill is pumped in an up-and-down fashion with the crossbar, which creates a fast spinning motion of the bit, reversing itself with each downward motion. Like the bow drill, the pump auger could be used for boring holes in either wood or metal by merely changing the bit, or even with the same bit as is the case with modern bits. The wooden flywheel acts to regulate and stabilize the speed.

SHOTGUN LOADING TOOL

This wooden tool was apparently used in connection with the reloading of shotgun shells. The peg at right was used to seat the primer cap before loading the shell, and the one at left was used to unseat the expended primer cap. It was acquired from Sevier County, Tennessee.

Scrap steel carefully saved for making gun parts by the Ottinger family.

Flintlock parts made from scrap in the old Ottinger gunshop.

When old John Ottinger came down the valleys from Pennsylvania into the wilderness of what is now Greene County, Tennessee, in the 1790's, he found that he was cut off from practically all sources of supplies. Some of the local foundries which were being built could supply some low grade iron, but good quality steel required for gun parts had to be secured from hundreds of miles away; and of course, there were no roads to these sources. It is little wonder, then, that every scrap of good steel had to be carefully saved.

When I purchased the remnants of the old Ottinger shop in 1978, I found a small box hidden beneath the work bench with what appeared to have been useless scrap. But closer inspection indicated that these bits and pieces were of the highest grade steel, suitable for making gun springs, triggers, etc.

The five pieces at left are broken and worn-out pieces of grain cradle blades and hay mowing blades. In the center are two worn-out files, used to make a variety of tools because of the high quality metal. In the upper right portion of the photograph are pieces of brass, probably intended for use as inlays.

In the photograph at right are various flintlock rifle parts, some of which were obviously made from scrap pieces such as those shown in the opposite photograph. The fact that the parts were for flintlocks indicates that Ottinger was active in gunmaking in the early 1800's, and perhaps earlier.

This old place which is located in the community of St. James at the foot of the Smoky Mountains has remained in the Ottinger family since old John died there at the age of 104. It is still owned by the Ottinger family.

CHAPTER VI
POWDER HORNS, POUCHES, CHARGERS, AND FLASKS

Gunpowder, which has been known to man for centuries, was made here in the southern mountains from materials available in the wilderness -- saltpeter, charcoal, and sulphur. A generally accepted mixture of the three components was seventy-five parts saltpeter, fifteen parts charcoal and ten parts sulphur.

Saltpeter, or potassium nitrate, was found in many caves of the area, and one can still find the remains of wooden vats used in processing of this important item. Although small amounts were extracted in pioneer times, many of the cave works were reactivated during the Civil War. John Sallings, who, according to the Guiness Book of World Records, was the oldest man ever to live in America, the second oldest person ever recorded, as well as the last survivor of the Civil War, told me that his task during part of the war was extracting saltpeter from caves on and near the Clinch River.

Charcoal was usually made from the willow tree, but other varieties of trees were preferred by some. My friend, Joe Diehl of nearby Knox County, has made gunpowder (and pursued about every other pioneer craft) since he was a boy. "I've tried just about everything that grows to make charcoal, and the best thing that I have ever found is the pith from cornstalks," Joe declared.

"Gunpowder made from the cornstalks is the cleanest burning powder you can get, and is almost smokeless. And it just makes better powder than you can get from willow or any of the other trees."

The third ingredient needed, and perhaps the hardest to come by in this area, was sulphur. Many wells in this region have sulphur water, and there are numerous sulphur springs. There is a community in this county named Sulphur Springs. This water can be boiled in large vats or kettles, leaving a residue of sulphur, in much the same manner as was used in "making" salt.

Several early powder "factories" sprang up in this area, one of the earliest being on Powder Branch near Erwin in Unicoi County, Tennessee. Tradition has it that this works furnished powder for the Tennesseans who crossed back over the mountains into North Carolina and fought in, and helped to win the famous battle of King's Mountain, called the battle that changed American history.

A few miles east of the Museum there is a community called Powder Springs where , I am told, gunpowder was made. And there was in later years (1905) a powder factory in this (Anderson) county some twelve miles west of the Museum at Marlow. Interestingly, this was located near Sulphur Springs, but I don't know whether this was coincidental. (My first experiment with making gunpowder was at the age of twelve -- a career which ended abruptly when my mother caught me burning some of my recently made product.)

Without gunpowder, the all important rifle was as useless as an ordinary club, and wet or damp powder was the same as no powder at all. For this reason, the container for storing and carrying it was of the utmost importance; and the horn from cattle became singularly suited for this purpose. The powder would not "draw" dampness inside as it would in metal containers, and yet the horn would repel the snow and rain indefinitely, an advantage over the cloth or leather containers. In addition, the curvature of the horn fitted perfectly the contour of one's side, just above the hip. It could be grasped conveniently when loading the rifle, the plug removed with one's teeth, and a portion of the contents poured from the small end into the powder measuring device called a charger. The plug, which remained in the teeth during this procedure, was then replaced, and the horn was allowed to fall into its original position, all within a few seconds.

Early powder horns in New England, New York and Pennsylvania, were often ornately engraved, decorated and signed. But fully ninety-five percent of the old horns I have found in the smokehouse and attics of Appalachia have been as plain and simple as the day they were sawed off the head of the family oxen, except for carved rings and knobs on the small end for the purpose of tying the carrying string. It is true that they were often gracefully shaped, but this was a natural feat, and credit is due to the cow, not the man who prepared it for use.

The inside core of the horn had to be removed before it was serviceable. This could be accomplished by boiling the horn for several minutes, whereupon the core became disengaged from the outer portion and could be removed through the large end of the

history.

horn, leaving only the thin shell. The horn could be flattened, or otherwise shaped after extended boiling.

Highly decorated brass, copper and pewter flasks have been used for storing and measuring powder for hundreds of years, but they were virtually never used on the frontier, especially not in this mountainous region. A few have been found, but they came mainly from the old landed gentry homes along the wide river valleys.

The powder chargers, the device for measuring one charge or load of powder, was traditionally made from the tip of a deer antler. But, as the illustrations will show, they were made of various other materials and were more apt to have some type of non-utilitarian carving than was the powder horn.

Almost as important as the horn and charger was the leather pouch, called a shot pouch or hunting pouch in this area. The frontier hunting pouches were often made of bearskin, or calf hide, and the leather was usually tanned without the hair being removed, as was often the case with saddlebags. I assume this was beneficial in repelling water in extended periods of rain and snow.

The pouch was used to carry the tow, wadding, bullets, flint, and other items and tools which the hunter might need. The pouches did not survive the generations of use as well as did the rifles and the horns, and, as a consequence, the early ones are quite rare -- much more so than are the rifles themselves.

POWDER SMOKE FROM THE KENTUCKY FLINTLOCK

Tony Denny of nearby Clinton is shown here at the Museum firing a flintlock Kentucky rifle using black powder. The small puff of smoke at the breech of the barrel is caused by the flint igniting the powder in the pan, which in turn ignites the powder inside the barrel, projecting the bullet and causing the smoke to escape at the muzzle. Tony Denny, an outdoor sportsman and a Kentucky rifle enthusiast, was killed in a motorcycle accident a few weeks after this photograph was taken by his father, and my long time friend, Wallace Denny.

STOOKSBURY POWDER HORN AND CHARGER

This powder horn is most typical of those found in the Southern Appalachian region -- plain, simple, yet serviceable and durable. Note the carved knob on the small end around which the string is tied. This, of course, is purely utilitarian and serves to prevent the rawhide from slipping off. The plug has a hole, once used to tie it to the horn so it would not be lost in the frenzy of reloading in the midst of killing a bear. The thong is cowhide.

The charger, carved from the tip of a deer antler, is unusual with its carved decoration. The checked carving is similar to its rifle companion described earlier. Note the lip carved into the open end, enabling one to more easily pour the powder into the muzzle of the rifle. These items came from Alfred Stooksbury of neighboring Union County, and had belonged to his grandfather, Alfred Boy Bledsoe, in the early 1800's.

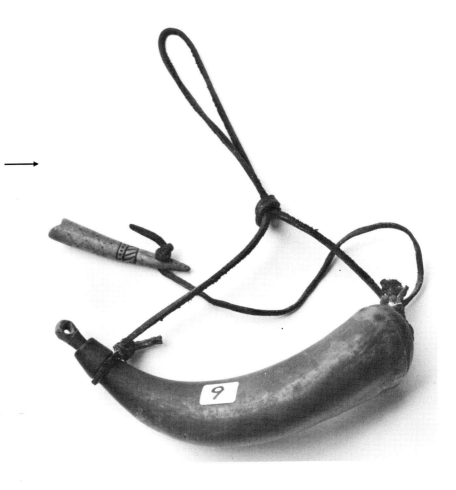

⟵ MONROE COUNTY HORN

The leather strap, from which the horn hung, is made from squirrel hide, which is home-tanned, using the old wood ash method. Note the worm damage on this horn, a condition one often finds in the old powder horns which have been stored in open sheds and smokehouses. The horn was purchased from the late Judge Roy Rogers of Monroe County, Tennessee, near the town of Madisonville. Note the wide groove carved in the small end to secure the leather thong.

DILLON HORN

←

It was from an old frontier-type log house that I purchased this old powder horn, about 1964, from a family named Dillon. It was located in southwestern Virginia in Scott County near the village of Rye Cove. I was informed that the original Dillons who settled there were ancestors of the famous marshal of Kansas. The horn has been carved, or scraped, leaving a double button type protrusion for holding the cord.

HODGE POWDER HORN →

This horn and the accompanying charger came from adjoining Knox County, Tennessee, with the Hodge rifle, pictured and discussed in Chapter I. The charger, made of deer antler, is the most ornately decorated one in the collection.

PREACHER EGAN HORN

This well-worn little horn came from the log smokehouse at the old Preacher Egan place near the community of Stanleytown in Scott County in southwest Virginia. This was a very old homestead and there were numerous frontier-pioneer type items there. I purchased the horn in 1963 from Eli Hackler, son-in-law of Egan.

VARMIT COUNTY HORN

A few miles west of the Museum in Campbell County, there is a remote mountainous area near the Kentucky-Tennessee line called "Varmit County". I don't know the derivation of the name unless it was because it was heavily populated by bears, panthers, and other varmints; wildcats are still found in that region. At any rate, that is the area from which this horn came. Note that the space between the two rings allows the thong to be tied between them, similar to the Dillon horn pictured on the opposite page.

LEFT-HANDED POWDER HORN

This horn has undergone little exterior change -- only a small groove has been carved on the tip to prevent the rawhide string from slipping off. The tip of the horn has apparently become splintered or cracked and for that reason cut off -- the string is now → tied to a staple. The unusual feature of this horn, which was acquired in nearby Claiborne County, is that it is shaped so as to be carried on one's left side, and was presumably used by a left-handed person.

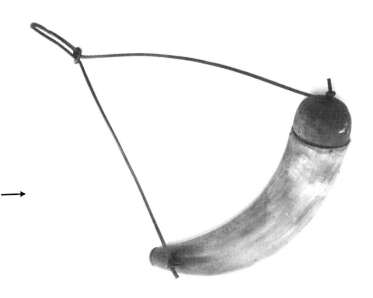

HACKWORTH HORN

This graceful powder horn was acquired from my friend, Glenn Hackworth, from one of this county's oldest and most picturesque areas, Dutch Valley, located some twelve miles west of the Museum. This valley was settled about 1800 by a group of Germans; hence the name Dutch, a corruption of the German "Deutsch".

EGAN FAMILY HUNTING GEAR ⟶

This early hunting bag, horn, and chargers were also from the old Egan homeplace. It, too, was acquired from Eli Hackler by my friend, W.G. Lenoir, from whom I bought it.

KNOXVILLE HUNTING BAG ⟶
AND POWDER HORN

This hunting bag, along with the powder horn and antler charger, was purchased from my old friend, Guy Bowers of Greeneville, about 1969 -- and he had bought it from "somewhere in Greene County." The leather hunting pouch has gold printing which reads "Will H. Gass, Knoxville, Tenn." I don't know whether Gass was the maker or the owner. Fragments of flint were found in the bag when I bought it; so I assume it had been used in connection with the flintlock. This would indicate that it might be quite old -- perhaps early 1800's.

The horn was apparently carefully selected as it has a most graceful shape and size, and the two concave rings have been expertly carved. Although these apparently originated in this region, they are not typical of the average mountain accessories.

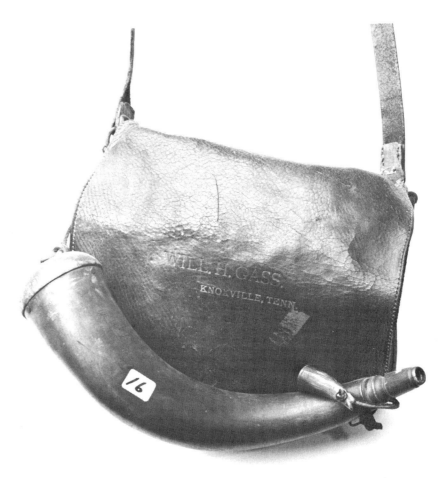

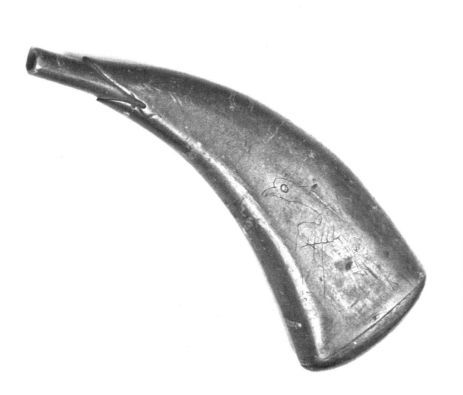

⟵ CARVED PRIMER HORN

This horn has apparently been boiled and flattened; and it has been carved in such a manner as to create a pouring tube inserted in the "fish's mouth." A crude likeness of a bird, an attempt at an eagle, I suppose, is carved on the opposite side. Although I acquired this unusual horn from a trader many years ago, I do not know that it originated in this region. But I have found two other horns with very similar mouths which came from this immediate area, an indication that this one also might be a "native."

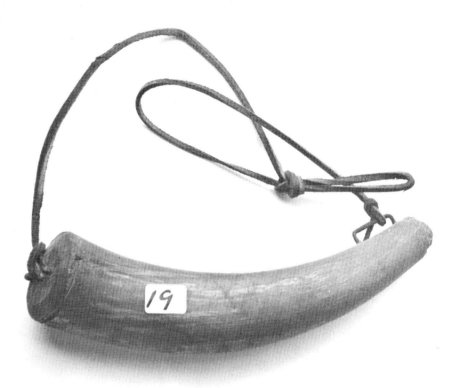

WASHINGTON COUNTY HORN AND CHARGER →

This horn, along with the brass charger, came from Washington County, Tennessee. This type indentation, carved on the end of the horn to secure the thong, is probably the most common type found in the region.

← ## KING KEATON HORN

I bought this little horn from King Keaton in 1969. King lived some fifteen miles south of Sneedville in Hancock County, Tennessee, on the old Henry Hutson place. Some of the oldest and rarest items in the Museum came from this old homestead. The tip of this horn has been broken off and the metal staple added for securing the rawhide string.

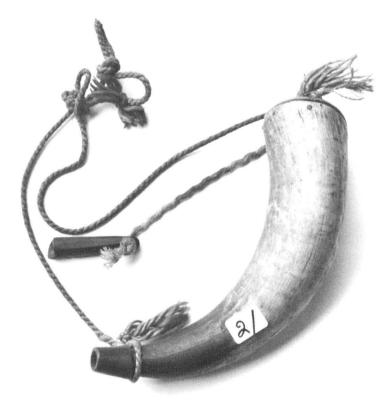

← ## CUMBERLAND COUNTY POWDER HORN

The decorated plug is rather unusual for a mountain horn; but its other features are quite typical of this region. The mouth of the original horn was probably damaged and consequently shortened, thus accounting for the metal staple for attaching the leather cord. The horn was purchased from my friend, Cobb Webb, of Crab Orchard in Cumberland County, Tennessee.

TWO RARE POWDER HORNS

The double powder horn shown in the top of the photograph is the only one I have found in this region. It has the carved ends and other characteristics of horns of Appalachia. I don't know the purpose for having two compartments, but it could have been to carry two different kinds of powder -- one section for the finer priming powder for flintlocks, for example. It came from Washington County in Upper East Tennessee, near Johnson City.

The flattened and carved horn was purchased from David Byrd, who has combed upper East Tennessee and the mountains of North Carolina for most of his life in search of early guns and related items. It came originally from Carter County, Tennessee.

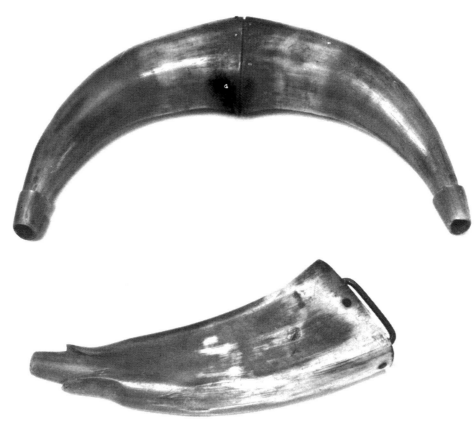

ROANE COUNTY HORN →

This interestingly carved horn, purchased in neighboring Roane County, Tennessee, in the mid sixties, is of a much later period than the others in the collection. The large plug, for example, has the acorn type knob carved onto it, a characteristic I never saw on the mountain horns of this region.

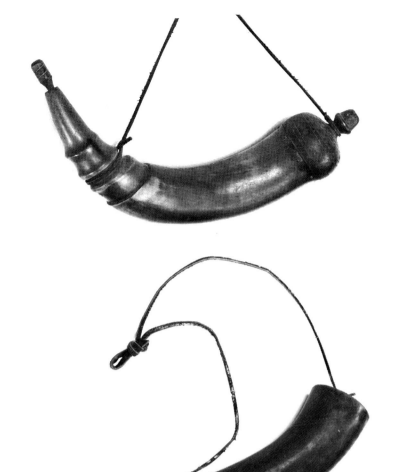

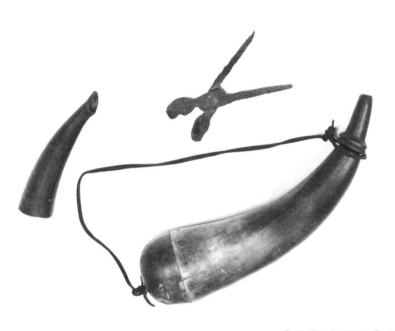

OLD KING POWDER HORNS

I bought these worn horns from Jason King the day before Christmas in 1973. He was then 99 years old and living in a little log house at the end of a mountain road in an isolated section of the Cumberland Mountains in adjoining Campbell County, Tennessee, in a section known as "Varmit County" (mentioned earlier) and more specifically in a hollow known as the King Settlement.

"I used them old horns most of my life", Jason told me, "til the cartridge gun came in a few years ago. And they belonged to my grandpap, James King. Now he was the first King ever to move into this wilderness country -- settled in here around 1840 and took up 700 acres of this wilderness country.

"Now they allus said that my grandpap kilt a hunnert bars (hundred bears) and he kilt them all with the old hog rifle -- using them old horns thar to carry his powder in."

James had nine children, giving them all biblical names such as John, Soloman, Issac, etc. Jason said his father was a "yarb (herb) digger, logger, farmer, hunter, and sich as that".

Although the generic nature of the two horns is similar in color, size and shape, there is a difference in the carving style. The horn at left has the double ring carving, while the other has the carved shoulder to secure the carrying string, both common to this region.

The bullet molds came from the Emory River area of Roane County, forty miles south of the Museum; and the funnel horn, presumably used for pouring powder into the horn, came from the old Sloan place on Notchie Creek, Monroe County, Tennessee, discussed earlier.

EAGLE HORN AND PRIMING HORNS

The winged eagle carved on the horn represents one of only two or three such types I have seen in Appalachia. As stated earlier such "art" work was common in the East and in other parts of the country, but seldom seen here in the mountains. It was acquired from David Byrd of Erwin, Tennessee.

The two smaller horns were called priming horns, and were used to carry a finer type powder used in the pan of the flintlock, which when fired, ignited the main charge inside the barrel. They were carried in the pouch; therefore they did not have the string or leather thong attached as did the regular horns.

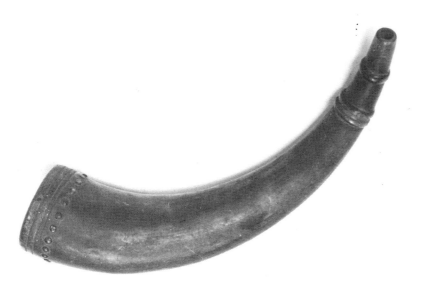

← SILL RICE POWDER HORN

This powder horn belonged to my grandfather, Marcellus Moss Rice, originally of Union County, but who lived most of his life on Bull Run Creek in adjoining Knox County, Tennessee. I assume that it originally belonged to one of his ancestors, probably his grandfather, George Rice, the gunmaker, or possibly pioneer James Rice, George's father, who settled Big Valley in the 1790's.

The brass tacks are for the purpose of holding the large walnut plug, but also served for aesthetic purposes. The small end has the double ring that held the carrying strap, with another single ring to prevent the string from slipping off.

BRASS POWDER FLASKS →

As indicated earlier, brass powder flasks were more traditionally used by the well-to-do folk and were not common in the mountains. However, some were found in the wide valleys and rich farming areas of Appalachia. The two small flasks were purchased from Mrs. R. L. Gaut of Bulls Gap in Green County, Tennessee. Mrs. Gaut, my longtime friend, along with her husband, was among the first to collect early relics in East Tennessee.

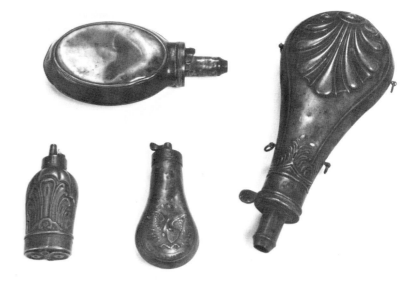

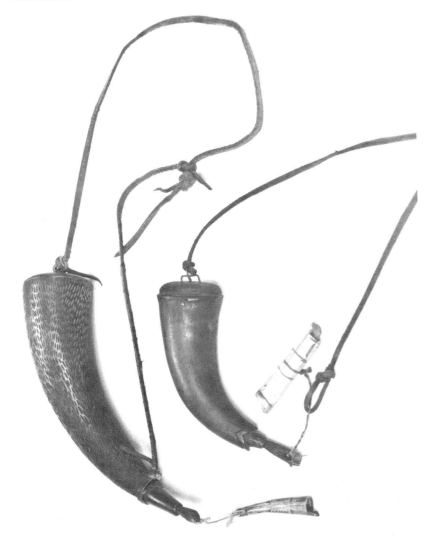

← FOLK ART POWDER HORNS

Both these horns were purchased from Everett Smith, my friend from Blount County, Tennessee, who spent many years buying Kentucky rifles in that area. The horn shown at top has hundreds of tiny slash marks burned into a sort of flowing pattern. The antler tip charger is also decoratively carved and has the tiny lip for pouring.

The small horn, probably for a flintlock, has the carved fish type mouth similar to several others in the Museum. The bone charger is divided in the center, and is in fact a double charger, one end being slightly larger for measuring a heavier load.

POWDER CHARGERS

The charger at left and the one at right are made of the tips of deer antlers, and both have the lips for pouring. The one shown second from left is made of river cane or reed, which once covered all the river and creek banks and low lands of this region and provided winter foliage for the buffalo and other large game. The charger shown third from the left is made of brass.

←

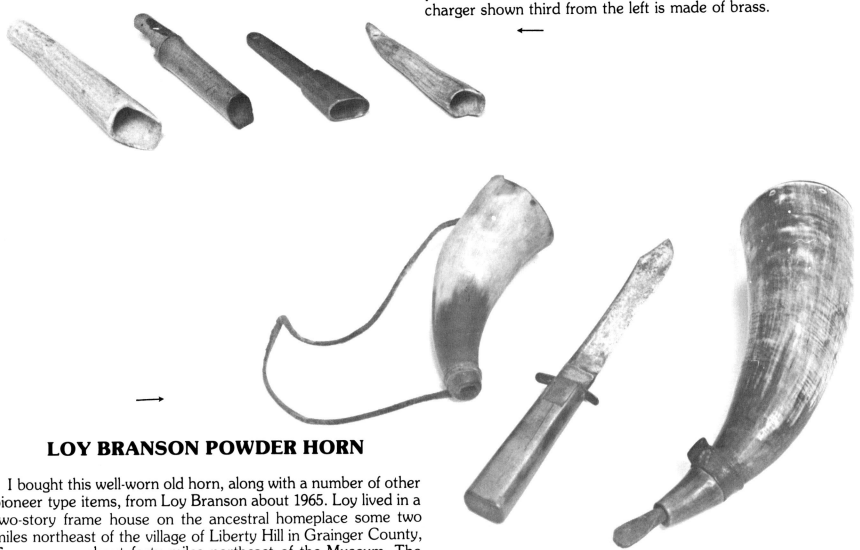

→

LOY BRANSON POWDER HORN

I bought this well-worn old horn, along with a number of other pioneer type items, from Loy Branson about 1965. Loy lived in a two-story frame house on the ancestral homeplace some two miles northeast of the village of Liberty Hill in Grainger County, Tennessee -- about forty miles northeast of the Museum. The primer horn is from Washington County, Tennessee, and the well-made bone-handled skinning knife came from the Smoky Mountain region.

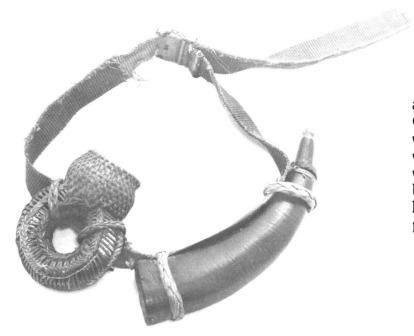

POWDER HORN - BULLET BASKET

←

These unusual items were purchased from David Byrd who acquired them from the Cherokee Indian section of North Carolina. The oddly-shaped, hand-woven basket-like container, which at one time probably had a lid made of the same material, was used, reportedly, to carry bullets. The same type material which appears to be native river cane, or reed, is used to attach the belt to the horn. Whether or not this was made in our area by the Indians, or whether other such devices were ever used, I do not purport to know.

→

LEATHER SHOT POUCHES

These leather pouches, used for carrying shot for the shotgun, represent the handmade and the factory made. The one at left is obviously one man's attempt at replicating the prestigious early factory made leather pouches such as the one shown at right.

The pouch at right is held upside-down with the tube inserted into the muzzle of the shotgun. When one presses the mechanism with the thumb, the front disc is raised, allowing the shot to pour into the barrel; but at the same instant the disc underneath the thumb is inserted into its slot cutting off the flow of shot so that a near exact measurement of the load can be made. For a slightly smaller load the front disc can be seated in the middle slot.

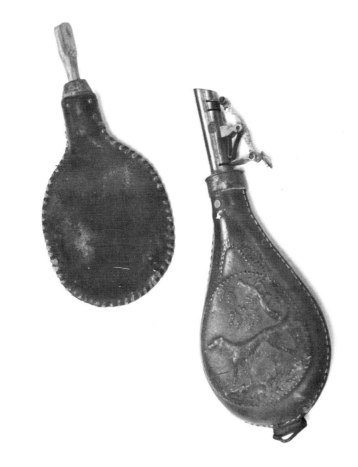

POWDER FLASKS

The brass powder flask at left has the traditional hunting dog scene embossed on its cover. The flask at right is made of what appears to be zinc.

THE "VALLEY" HORN AND THE "MOUNTAIN" HORN →

The larger well-scraped and polished horn came from the fertile farmland region of Washington County, Tennessee, while the crudely-made smaller one is from a mountain homestead in the isolated county of Hancock. The large horn has a walnut plug which has been turned on a lathe and has decorative graduated circles. It has been scraped very thin, and has a deep sheen. The plug used as the stopper is an old fiddle-tuning peg. The small horn was purchased from King Keaton, discussed earlier, who lived on the old Hutson place near Clinch River and about fifteen miles south of Sneedville, Tennessee.

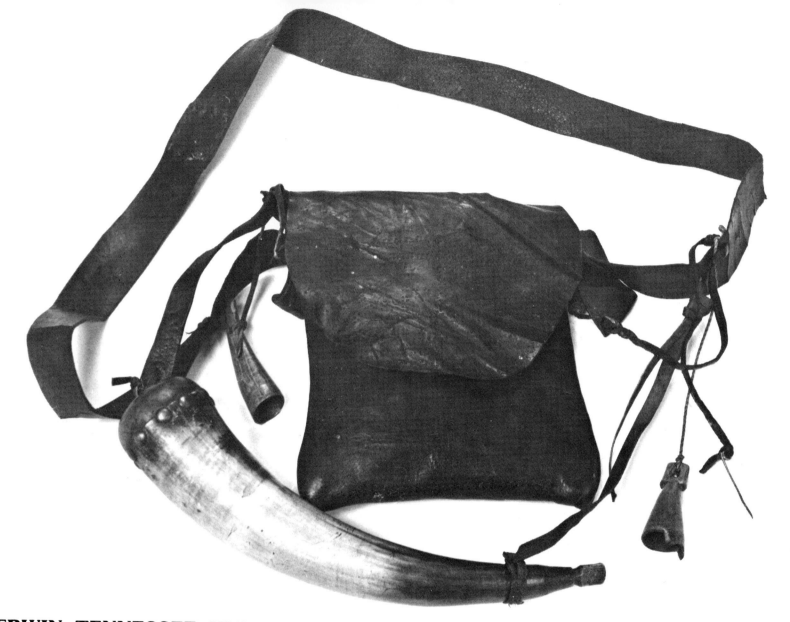

ERWIN, TENNESSEE, HUNTING GEAR

It is not often that one finds hunting regalia from the frontier period in such good condition. This hunting pouch, the horn, and the chargers are as serviceable today as they were when they were hung up from their last hunt. (The charger at left is made of horn while the one at right is of walnut.) These items were acquired from David Byrd of Erwin, Tennessee.

PIONEER POWDER GOURDS

In a land of little iron, glass or china, the gourd was used for all types of containers; and their use for the storage of powder was no exception. They were waterproof, did not "draw" dampness, and they could be grown the first season the family spent in the wilderness. The powder was presumably stored in the gourd, and then poured in the powder horn for the hunting trip.

The small well-worn gourd at left was acquired from the Everett Smith collection, mentioned earlier, from Blount County, and the large one shown in the center was purchased from David Byrd.

The small powder gourd at right was purchased, along with several pioneer relics, from the old Floyd Farmer place located in Block House Valley twelve miles south of the Museum. The homeplace had belonged to Floyd's father, Isaac, and had been in the possession of the Farmer family since the early days of the settlement of that area. The post office, which served the Farmer family in the early days, but which has long since been discontinued, was "Bud". Some of the old letters were addressed to the Farmers at Bud, Tennessee.

Lead for bullets was available in limited quantities in Southern Appalachia and was eagerly sought and highly valued. An area a few miles north of the Museum in Union County is called "Lead Mine Bend" for its rich deposits of lead. Pat Alderman of Erwin, Tennessee, in his account of the Battle of Kings Mountain, mentions lead being mined from a hill on the Nolichucky River in 1780.

Joe Diehl, discussed earlier in connection with gunpowder, who has spent much time in geological quests in the East Tennessee area, states that he has found numerous lead deposits. "Lead is found in the dolomite stone -- and I can tell by the looks of the rock and by the type of formation whether there's apt to be lead there or not," Joe says.

"You can tell by the feel if there's lead in the rock, and if you find it you just crush the rock or break it with a hammer and melt it down. When you get it melted the pure lead will pour from the bottom, and all the impurities will rise to the top."

My friend, Gene Purcell, who has probably done more archelogical excavation than anyone in this entire region, reminds me that lead was dug near his home some seven miles south of the Museum at a place near Clinch River called the Dismal Bluff. Civil War soldiers were quartered there for mining the lead, and the operations continued on into the 1880's.

The process of making bullets is quite simple. The lead is melted (at 621 F.) in small iron pots and dipped out with a large spoon-like dipper called a ladle and then poured into the cavity of the bullet mold through a tiny opening between the two sections. The lead solidifies almost instantly in the mold, which works like a pair of common pliers. The mold is then opened, allowing the bullet to be removed. The spur, which is formed in the opening through which the lead is poured, must be cut off, and the process is completed The bullet itself is slightly smaller than the bore of the rifle (about five thousandths of an inch) to allow for the patch around which the bullet is wrapped.

As the following photographs indicate, the type, shape and individuality of the bullet molds and ladles in this area varied greatly. And the materials from which the molds were made included stone and wood, as well as metal.

Since there was no standard size used for the bore of the mountain-made rifle, the rifle maker, or its owner, had to make a mold for each rifle. It probably took much less time to make blank molds than it did to make the cherry for cutting the mold cavity. The steel sphere had to be filed into a series of cutting edges, and it had to be tempered in such a manner as to drastically harden the metal. Since the rifle bore had to be redressed periodically, some say after firing a hundred rounds, the bore of the rifle became larger over a period of time, and correspondingly the mold size had to be increased. This often required making a larger cherry.

THE VERY LARGE AND THE SMALL

The mold on the right is about the average size of those used for making bullets for the old muzzle loaders. From the comparison, one can appreciate the size of the large handmade one shown at left. I acquired it about 1965 from the Schultz family of the Dutch Valley section of this county, and I feel that it was made in that area.

MAKING A BULLET MOLD

Matt Owenby is shown here in his shop in the Glades Community of Sevier County, Tennessee, about 1936, demonstrating how he made a bullet mold. In the left photograph he demonstrates how the blank was forged on the anvil, and at right he is reaming out the mold portion by hand, using a reamer, or cherry. Note the ancient pump bellows he used to force air into his forge, and the clay used for sealing the muzzle end of the bellows. (Photos courtesy of Ed Trout and the Great Smoky Mountains National Park)

MAKING BULLETS

Here the lead is melted in the large three-legged pan from which it is dipped with the lead ladle. From the ladle the lead is poured into the cavity of the mold and the bullet is formed almost instantly.

The unusual melting pan came from the old Ottinger place near the village of St. James in Greene County, Tennessee, discussed earlier in Chapter V in connection with gunmaking tools. This homestead was settled in the late 1700's and has been owned by the Ottinger family ever since. The two lead pots shown at left are of the more common type used in molding bullets.

WOODEN BULLET MOLDS

These rare items illustrate the individuality and ingenuity of the mountain people. The mold at right is made of hickory and the cavity is lined with what appears to be babbitt. If the bare wood were left exposed the hot lead would probably char it over a period of time, causing an enlargement of the hole, which in turn would cause the bullet to become larger and unable to fit into the gun barrel.

I bought this long-handled mold from Guy Bowers of Greeneville about 1968. He bought it, he told me, from "old Blind Jim Cagle" of Greene County in the 1930's.

The wooden mold at left is lined with beeswax. This may have been for the purpose of providing a film of wax on the bullet so it would more freely exit the rifle, but this is conjecture. The small hole on the inside of the handle serves as a guide - the other handle having a peg which fits into this hole, making sure the two parts of the mold are matched properly. This mold was purchased from Lee Hill of nearby Tazewell, Tennessee, who acquired it from an old mountain home near there.

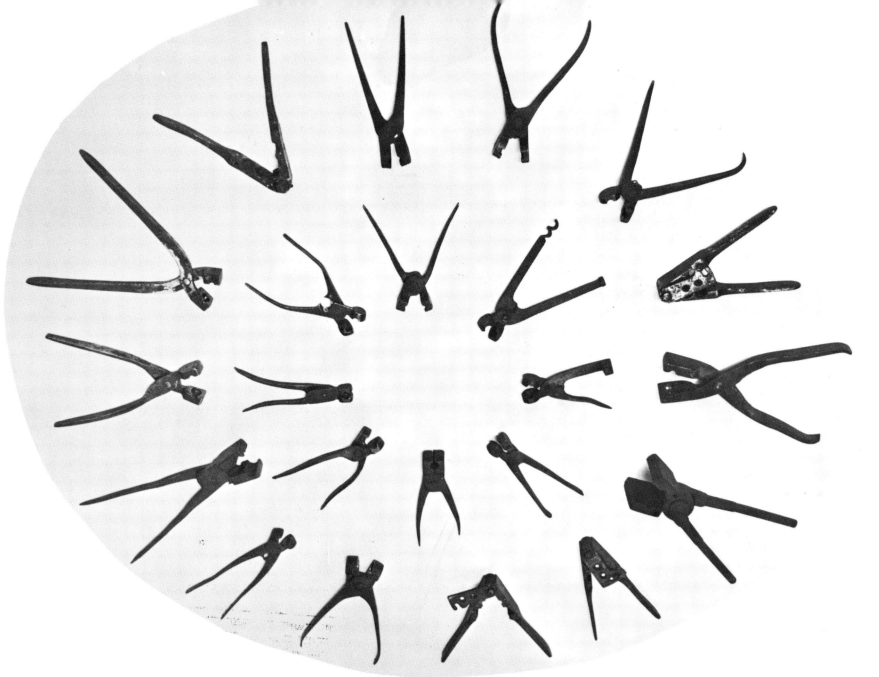

NO TWO BULLET MOLDS SEEMED EVER TO BE THE SAME

The varied collection of bullet molds was acquired for the Museum from my friend, Everett Smith of the East Tennessee community of Louisville in Blount County. For many years, Everett collected Kentucky rifles and various associated items from this area, during which time he accumulated this assortment of molds.

AM HACKWORTH MOLDS →

The average size Kentucky rifle bullet mold shown at left is contrasted to the two large, early factory molds. The one shown in the center has the capacity of producing six bullets. It, along with the one shown at right, belonged to Am Hackworth, a native of Dutch Valley in this (Anderson) county, and who died about 1977 at the age of 100 years. They were purchased from his son Everett. (Photo by the author)

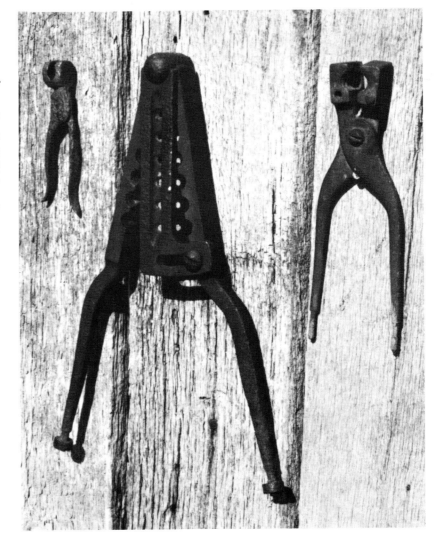

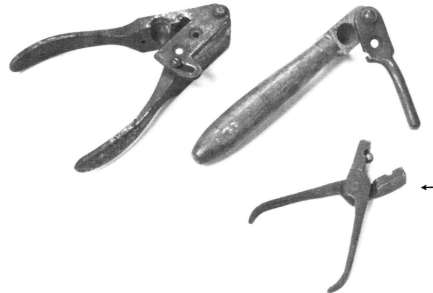

← The double mold at left can produce both the conical and the spherical-shaped bullet. The cover, when moved to the side, cuts the spurs off the bullets, a chore which had to be done by hand with the old type molds.

The mold shown in the center is the only one I have ever seen, I believe, with only one handle. Here again, the swivelcover trims the protruding spur as it is moved to the open position. The small mold to the right is a typical early Kentucky rifle mold.

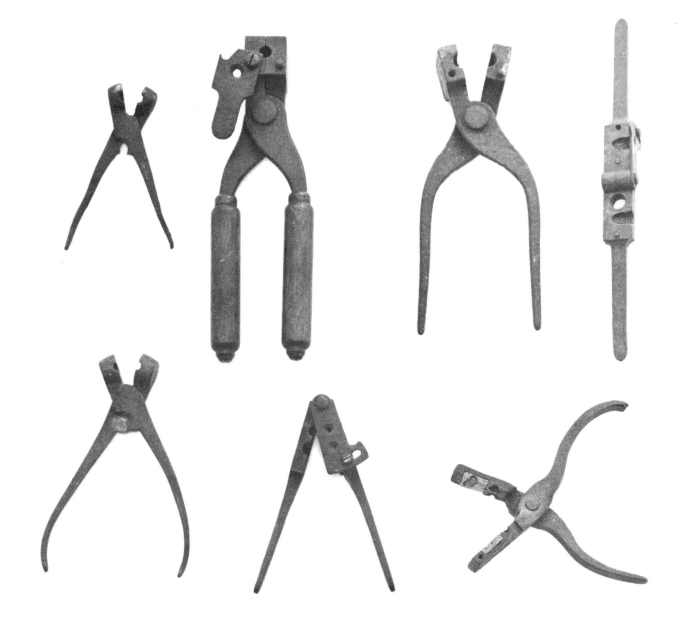

The bullet molds in this photograph show the seemingly endless types of styles. The one shown at lower right was acquired from the gunmaker, Charlie Blevins, pictured and discussed earlier. Note that he has converted it to produce a different size and shaped bullet by doing away with the original mold portion and then inserting brass linings with openings of the size desired.

BULLET MOLDS AND LOADING TOOLS

Although these bullet molds and loading tools were factory made, and were not associated with the muzzle-loading Kentucky rifle, they were collected in this area and they represent something of the transitional era in weaponry in Appalachia.

STONE BULLET MOLD

The stone mold shown here enables one to make a 38-caliber bullet, and a dozen shot with a single filling. I acquired this rare piece from my collector friend, Dr. William Acuff of Knoxville. He purchased it in western North Carolina, but its precise origin is unknown.

The cherry inserted in the brace illustrates how the cavity was made by the turning of the grooved head of the cherry inside the mold. The smaller photograph shows the mold in its closed position ready for the pouring of the lead.

BULLET MOLD CHERRIES

When inserted in a brace and turned, the cherry would cut a cavity in which the bullet could be molded. The size of the cavity and the caliber of the bullet, of course, corresponded precisely to the size of the cutter head on the cherry. These tools, made from old files, rasps and other scrap metal were collected over a period of many years by David Byrd in and around his home in Unicoi County, Tennessee, and in the mountains of Western North Carolina.

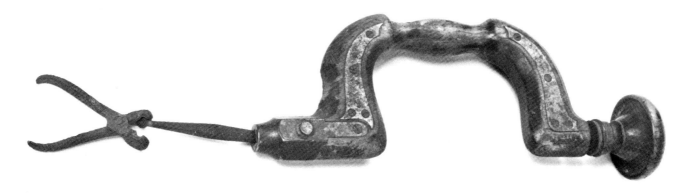

The above photograph illustrates how the cherry was employed to make the cavity in an early type Kentucky rifle mold. In actual practice the jaws of the mold would be closed so that the cherry would cut into both sections at equal speed.

SHOT MOLD

Shot for shotguns has long been made by pouring molten lead from a height which separates as it falls and cools, forming tiny shot; the higher one is from the ground, the smaller the shot which are formed. But everyone did not have a shot tower and the means of producing the shot in quanity, hence the purpose of this shot mold.

HANDMADE LEAD LADLES

Some perceptive people may recognize the ladle at left as having been fashioned from a buggy step. I purchased it from Ermon Sloan, a descendant of the gunmaking Sloans in Monroe County discussed earlier. It was made by Ermon's grandfather, James Riley Sloan, a farmer, blacksmith, and Civil War veteran who lived on Cagle Creek, a few miles east of Madisonville.

The ladle shown in the center was acquired from the late King Keaton, mentioned earlier in connection with powder horns. The ladle at right was purchased from my long-time friend, the late Peck Wilson, who was reared in this county. The fact that the handle was so short probably required the wooden attachment for insulation against the heat from the metal.

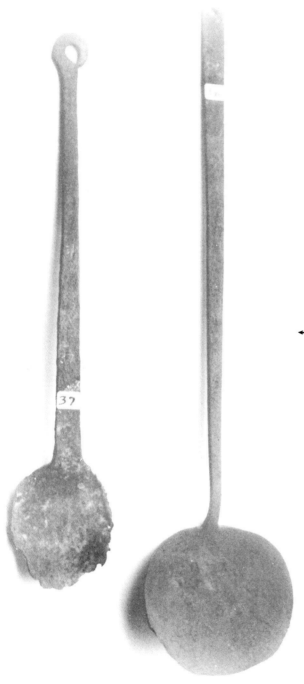

WILEY BONHAM LADLE →

This ladle was acquired from Wiley Bonham of near Jonesville, in Lee County, Virginia. It is from his father's old blacksmith shop which was located on Town Creek in Jonesville. The circular form created at the handle end is quite common on ladles, iron spoons, and shovels, and more carefully made pieces. In addition to its aesthetic value, this feature also provides a means of hanging the ladle.

← GREENE COUNTY LADLES

The ladle at left came from the old Dr. Rader place near the village of Bulls Gap, Tennessee, in Greene County, from a farm settled about the time of the American Revolution. The ladle was purchased from Harold Rader, a descendant who still owns the homeplace which has never been sold. (Bulls Gap's claim to fame is that it is the home of "Hee Haws," Archie Campbell.

The long-handled ladle on the right was reportedly made by an old blacksmith named Melvin Hartman who lived in a community called Hartman's Chapel, also in Greene County, Tennessee. It was purchased from Paul Wellborn who lives in the Hartman's Chapel Community.

CHAPTER VIII
THE MOUNTAIN CROSSBOW

The late Dr. Norbert Riedl, an anthropology professor from the University of Tennessee, was one of the first to take an interest in my collection and remained a frequent visitor to the Museum until his untimely death. When he saw the early crossbow I brought in, he was amazed and excited, and said: "Of the 40,000 items in the Museum, this crossbow is probably the most significant single item." And, although one could make a similar claim for many artifacts, I could not disagree with Bert.

None of my research, nor any of the commentaries I have read relative to the pioneer-frontier period of our country, mentions the crossbow as having been used in early America. My friend, Gene Purcell, one of the most astute observers of our early culture and one who has done extensive excavation of the early ruins in Appalachia, points out that there have been objects discovered which suggest to some that crossbows were used in the Revolutionary period. Others disagree. Robert Johnson, owner-operator of the Museum, "Whistle In The Woods" in Rossville, Georgia, thinks the crossbow was used early in New England and later in the Pacific Northwest, but had never heard of it being used in Appalachia. Even DeSoto's men, coming into this region in the 1540's, 200 years before the first settlers arrived, had largely converted to the use of guns.

But there it was, a genuine early crossbow -- doubtless of the 1700 period or earlier and it was found in Green County, Tennessee. I began to inquire in that area and a couple of the old men recalled seeing the remnants of "old-timey crossbows when they were young. I asked Alex Stewart, the old mountain man I consult when all other inquiries fail. "Why Lordy, yes", he said, "I recollect hearing tell of the crossbow. My Grandpap Stewart had one that I can recollect seeing when I's a boy. And the folks back before my time hunted with them. They's so poor they couldn't get hold of a rifle gun, and if they did it was hard to get powder and lead. If a feller back then had a gun, he's big man."

In recent years I have found several older folk in isolated areas who remembered hearing of the use of crossbows as a hunting weapon. I asked Alex how effective the crossbow was in hunting. "Why a man could hunt right along with a good hunting bow. You take one that's made jest right, why pshaw, you could kill a deer or bear, or just about anything you'd come across. Of course, they wuz used mainly to hunt small game -- rabbits, squirrels, and sich as that -- and fish. Yes sir, them people up on Newman's Ridge could never have made it way back yonder if it hadn't been fer having the crossbows."

I asked Alex about the technique of making a crossbow and the type wood used. "Well, they generally used poplar for the stock. It's light and yet it's strong. But black haw is the best for the bow if you can find it -- but cedar will do if you get the right mixture of red and white. And hickory makes a good arrie (arrow) -- it is straight grained and won't hardly break."

Since I had found no pioneer artifact which Alex could not make from scratch, I asked him if he thought he could make a crossbow. And with a response as quick and confident as Harry Truman's, he said, "Why shore -- if I can get the timber."

We did get the timber and Alex had soon completed the task. It took all of one's strength to bend the thin bow back to the cocked position, and when we "pushed" the trigger, the arrow sped out with such speed that it was barely discernable -- an unbelievably deadly weapon.

The crossbow was developed in the medieval period and mechanized as early as the 1400's by the addition of a two-handled windless to draw the bow into the shooting position. But the crossbow Alex made was more simplistic and void of any metal.

Since we could not find a suitable haw tree, Alex used cedar for the bow. It has the proper ratio of white and red, a combination absolutely necessary for creating the proper spring and strength.

The weapon is cocked by pulling the bow back and catching the bow string on a notch cut near the handhold of the stock. The arrow lies in a groove cut into the stock so that when the string is released by the trigger, the bow almost instantaneously springs to its original position driving the arrow out the groove at almost bullet speed. (I believe that most of the old crossbows had a thin wood covering over the groove to keep the arrow from riding upward as it sped out.) The trigger consists of a six-inch long piece of wood dislodging the string from its catch.

I have acquired every crossbow I have found, a total of only five, which are shown pictured on the following pages. Although they were acquired from various areas in Southern Appalachia, all of these crossbows have remarkably basic similarities.

Alex Stewart and his Home Made Crossbow

Alex Stewart, in his late eighties, is shown here with a crossbow he made for the Museum. "I recalled my Grandpap's old crossbow that he used for huntin' when I's jest a boy and we lived on top of Newman's Ridge", Alex told me. "They wasn't no guns to speak of -- if they wuz it was hard to get the powder and lead."

In the center picture, Alex shows the groove into which the arrow is placed, and in the third photo the trigger can be seen. The bow string is released by pushing the trigger forward, which raises the top portion of the trigger "mechanism", pushing the string out of its notched "seat". (Photo by the author)

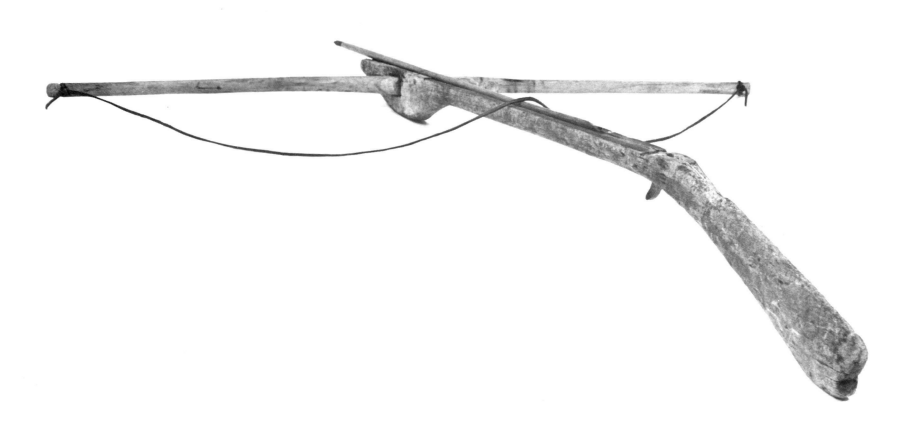

EARLY GREENE COUNTY CROSSBOW

The late Norbert Riedl, well-known anthropologist with the University of Tennessee, stated that this crossbow was the most significant single item in the entire Museum. To our knowledge this was the first clue that the crossbow, indeed, may have been used by the pioneers of this region.

Although the stock is made of poplar, it is remarkably similar to the 1700 flintlock rifle stock. The trigger and the thin covering appear to be original. I spent many hours replacing the bow of red cedar, but it snapped the first time I tried to cock it. I made the mistake of not retaining any white or sap portion on the bow, hence it had no spring or resiliency.

Guy Bowers found this rare weapon in his native Greene County in the 1930's in what he called "the old Dutch (German) Settlement." It took me many years to purchase it, and then only because I had "bought so many things for so many years."

NORTH CAROLINA CROSSBOW

⟵

This pine crossbow was purchased from Ruby Warren of Candler, near Asheville. Although she stated that it came from the mountainous section of Western North Carolina, Ruby could not give me any more specific information as to its origin.

The cover is quite massive and appears to be more a part of the weapon than that on the two crossbows just discussed. It is interesting that the wooden trigger has been replaced here with one similar to a gun trigger. It is pulled rather than pushed, and it even has a trigger guard. The bow is missing.

BUNCOMBE COUNTY, NORTH CAROLINA CROSSBOW ⟶

When I bought the contents of the little Tweed Museum, located between Asheville and Weaverville, I discovered this crossbow. It is obviously the "youngest" one illustrated here, but like the one from Ruby Warren (which was acquired only a few miles away) it has a metal trigger and trigger guard. The brass heart decorations are reminiscent of the silver, copper, and brass inlays found on some of the Kentucky rifles.

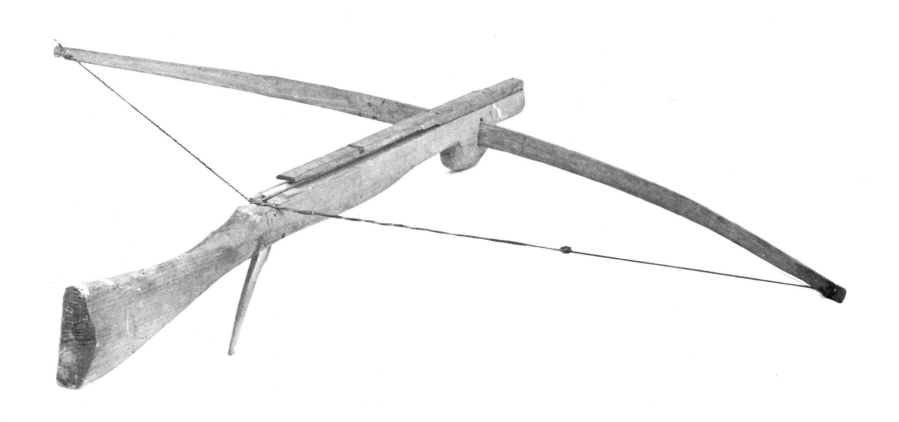

FALL BRANCH CROSSBOW

I acquired this crossbow a few miles north of Greeneville, home of Guy Bowers from whom the very old crossbow was purchased. This one, bought from Paul Ryan who has "turned up" thousands of very old and fine relics, is obviously not nearly as old as the one from Guy. However, it has several similar features. It has the cover over the arrow, and the trigger is pushed forward for release. (Note the arrow protruding from under its cover.)

ADDENDUM TO THE FIRST EDITION

Since the completion of *Guns and Gunmaking Tools of Southern Appalachia* three years ago, I have acquired additional relics and photographs related to the subject. Rather than reorganize the entire book and insert these photographs and this information in the respective appropriate places, they are being included at the end of the book as an addendum, or a sort of postscript, but with tie-in references made to the proper chapter and topic.

THE SQUIRREL RIFLE

As has been pointed out previously, the Kentucky Rifle was almost always called a hog rifle, or squirrel rifle by the old folk of the Southern Appalachian mountains. For this reason, and because of the squirrel carving on the stock, we classify this as a squirrel rifle. It is a good example of a crudely made, though serviceable, mountain rifle. I acquired it from an old homeplace in Washington County, in upper East Tennessee, near Johnson City. (Photo by the author)

LUTHER GRAVES AND HIS SCRATCH SHOTGUN

Almost daily one hears television commercials extolling the virtues of various products because they are made from "scratch". One such commercial has gone so far, using the metaphor incorrectly, as to claim the biscuits taste "just like scratch".

"Made from scratch" connotes made from the basics and probably relates back to the pioneer foot races which started from a line "scratched" in the dirt; hence starting from scratch, is starting from the beginning.

Few people would argue that Luther Graves' shotgun was not made from scratch, although it is of quite recent vintage. The stock is from a scrap piece of pine, the barrel is made from a half inch pipe, the butt plate from the leather sole of a worn out shoe, and the mechanical parts are undefinable bits and pieces of scrap metal. There are a number of screws used in the construction, and no two are alike. By chance or by design it accommodates a 410 shell and has never mis-fired.

One slight disadvantage with this weapon is that the barrel must be completely removed from the stock in order to load it, a process which takes slightly longer than it did to load the old Kentucky rifle. The applied trigger and trigger guard is completely superfluous since the firing pin is released by triggering a device on top of the stock.

But then Luther, who lives alone in the tiny three-room house he built for himself over the years, was not trying for perfection. He's one of twenty-six children, of pioneer stock, and he still has some self-reliant ingenuity. He's played music for as long as I can remember, but he never expected any pay; he makes wooden airplanes and other crafts and gives them all away; and he has an old building which he has converted to a barber shop, but he has never charged for a haircut. He doesn't look his 78 years, and fully expects to live to be 105, the age of his grandfather when he died.

Luther admitted that he made the shotgun "just to have something to be doin'," and readily agreed to sell it to me. I subsequently loaned it to the Folklife section of the World's Fair in Knoxville where it was viewed by millions of people from throughout the world. It is now on permanent display at the Museum of Appalachia.

Luther is shown here in the "front" room of his humble abode with the gun; and in the photograph below he demonstrates how the barrel is unscrewed for loading. (Photo by Gary Hamilton)

NORTH MISSISSIPPI GUNSHOP RIFLE

Emmet Keeton, who lived near Booneville, in the northeast corner of Mississippi, a few miles from the famous Natchez Trace, made and used this dummy rifle as a sign for his gunshop. The author is shown holding the double barrel "Weapon" in the Museum of Appalachia gun display. (Photo by Bob Kollar)

HACKER MARTIN'S UNFINISHED AXLE RIFLE

If the deprivation of the mountains fostered resourcefullness, ingenuity and analytical thought, then Hacker Martin is a choice representative of these attributes. He is discussed throughout the book (see index) and was one of this country's best known Kentucky rifle makers during his lifetime.

He knew that annealing, the heating and subsequent cooling of steel, softened and hopefully improved it's quality. He also was familiar with the retort buggies used by the giant Tennessee Eastman Company in nearby Kingsport, in connection with making charcoal. He reasoned that the steel axles of these buggies were constantly subjected to extreme heat, followed by cooling. If this was good for metal, then certainly the axles from these buggies would be in fine condition for making gun barrels.

So, Hacker made arrangements with a friend to secure one of these axles, and they formed a sort of partnership for the purpose of making what they hoped would be an exceptional rifle. Hacker reportedly bored the axle, and had it planed to an octogon shape, and prepared it for firing. It was during the test-firing stage, and before the stock was completed, that the partnership dissolved, ostensibly because of some disagreement, and Hacker's partner ended up with the unfinished piece. Some years later it was bought by J.H. Moran of Kingsport, and it was from Moran that I acquired it in 1981. The barrel of this unusual piece is 48 inches long, and its weight is an unbelievable 40 pounds.

The writer's daughter Elaine Irwin Meyer, and granddaughter Lindsey are shown with the heavy, unfinished weapon at one of the log houses at the Museum of Appalachia. (Photo by Ed Meyer)

OSCAR BLEVINS—PIONEER IN THE 20TH CENTURY

The calendar indicated that the year was 1981, but all other indicators said it was early times in frontier America. The place was near Leatherwood Ford on the Big South Fork River at the border of two East Tennessee mountainous counties—Fentress and Scott. The few miles from Oneida took over an hour and the roads became so bad that I began to wonder if they were ever intended for a motor car. Miles were traveled without seeing a single house, and the mountains got more precipitous until finally I came upon the beautiful Big South Fork River appearing, I thought, precisely as it did when the first white man set foot there. Across the river and half a mile up a steep ridge, and finally in a clearing in the forest I found the Oscar Blevins homestead.

This was the region that produced men like Sgt. Alvin C. York, called the greatest hero of World War I. Cordell Hull, who served a record-breaking term as Secretary of State and whose accomplishments rival any American's in this century, was born and raised one county over. The title "Father of the United Nations" is but one of his many honors. And less than ten miles away the parents of Mark Twain left for Missouri a few months before the famous writer was born.

There was no telephone here, nor electricity, and the water was carried from a spring a quarter mile away. Wild animal skins hung drying in the wood-shed, a deer stand was located near the edge of the clearing, potatoes were buried, pioneer fashion, in the garden, and a wildcat cage sat on a block of oak near the front porch.

Oscar is descended from the legendary Blevins men who came into the wilderness with Daniel Boone and the long hunters. He is a nephew of Charlie Blevins, discussed extensively in the body of this volumn. (See index) For seven years the government men had been giving him yes and no answers about taking his land for the Big South Fork National River and Recreational Area, and

Oscar Blevins demonstrates how he used the bow and iron gig for spearing fish in the nearby Big South Fork River. (Photo by Gary Hamilton)

he was understandably angry. "One of them giverment men will tell me I'll have to go, and the next week another one will say they've changed their minds. Hit's been that away for seven years. I never know whether to put out a crop, and if I do I don't know whether they'll let me stay to gather it or not. They jest keep me tore up all the time."

Oscar was a typical mountain man, fiercely honest, neighborly, proud and independent, highly intelligent, and I suspected quick tempered. If he liked me I would have had no worry about trusting my life to him. But I wouldn't sleep well if he was really angry with me.

Over a period of months I bought several early relics from Oscar, and one day I noticed what appeared to be an arrow resting on the porch wall-plate. On closer examination I found it really was an arrow, but to my astonishment it did not have the usual single spike, but rather a three-tined gig. "Why, that's the way we done our fishing down here in the river. I've killed a many a fish with that spear and a bow—Lord, yeah, a wagon wouldn't hold the fish we've killed with that!"

Here in the 20th Century, in the United States, was the same type fishing method which man had used several thousands of years ago. A few weeks later I received a long letter from one G.H. Winston of Green Bay, Virginia, complimenting me on *Guns and Gunmaking Tools of Southern Appalachia.* A portion of his letter reads as follows:

> "The information on crossbows astounded me and this is probably the true contribution of your book to the world. I read something, and for the life of me I can't remember where, but it was within the last five years of the account of a traveler in the Southern Appalachia mountains in the latter part of the 1870's. This man went into the remote region, never visited by outsiders, and saw an old man shooting fish with a bow and arrow."

Well, if this was a spectacular scene in the 1870's, it is even more remarkable in the 1980's. The iron gig was made by one of Oscar's uncles who, like many members of the Blevins family, was a blacksmith as well as a gunsmith. Oscar sold me the red cedar bow and a couple of arrows with single spikes, but he wanted to hold on to the three-tined gig for a while; and I could certainly understand that.

On one of my subsequent visits Oscar talked about his family's history. The following information is precisely as taken from the tape recorder and demonstrates Oscar's spontaneous recall of his family's history.

"The first Blevins that ever come into this country was my great, great grandfather. He was born in 1779, I believe. And he come in here when he was a young man. He come from Pulaski County, Kentucky—he come through Cumberland Gap. He come first to Pulaski County then on down to Wayne County, what we call Oil Valley over there, and settled a while, then he come on through to Rock Creek, then he come on through to No Business and lived a while. He hunted.

"When he come in here he had one of them ole hog (Kentuckey) rifles and he would carry his fry pan with him. His name was Johathan Blevins, and he's buried over here on Station Camp."

DID HE HAVE A FAMILY WHEN HE CAME INTO THIS REGION?

"Well, I think he married after he came in this country (vicinity). He had been married in Kentucky and his wife died there. He come on in here and married and lived on Station Camp over here and he died in 1863."

AND JONATHAN WAS YOUR GREAT GRANDFATHER?

"He wuz my great, great grandfather. My great grandfather was buried right up here at this cemetery beside the road. He was buried over there in 1868, but he was only 57 years old when he died. He died in September, I believe it was, of '68. His name was Jacob Blevins.

"He wuz livin' across the road from the cemetery right out the road here, and he got sick and wuz a draggin' around. And he got him a stick and went across the road and drove that stick into the ground to see how deep the ground was—to see if it was deep enough (without hitting rock) for a grave. He left the stick there and went on back to the house and never did get well. And when he died they buried him right where he drove that stick and that was the startin' of that cemetery."

WHAT IS THE NAME OF THE CEMETERY?

"Hit's called the Katie Blevins Cemetery. Jacob's wife's name was Cath-er-ryn, and they jest shortened it and called her Katie. And she lived on a long time after he died and they got to burying people there and they got to calling it the Katie Blevins Cemetery because she lived there at the place. Now my grandfather Jake, he came back home after his daddy died and lived there til he died.

DID MOST OF THE BLEVINS' MAKE GUNS?

"Yes, they wuz all gunmakers, I reckon."

ARE THERE ANY OF THE OLD BLEVINS' GUNS STILL AROUND?

After a long pause he said, "Not many." I then suspected that he had one and like many people nowadays, did not want it known for fear it would be stolen.

Finally, I said, "Oscar, I bet you've got one hid away back there in the bedroom?" After that, much laughter from him and his wife. And finally he said, "Now, you ain't supposed to ask no such questions." This was followed by much more laughter. Then he said to his wife: "Get that powder horn over thar, and I'll get the old gun".

Oscar parted the curtains that hung over the doorway leading into the back room and disappeared only for a minute. Then he came out proudly displaying the fine old Kentucky rifle made by his grandfather Jake Blevins. The gun was a fine specimen, but the hunting pouch, horn, and charger were the finest examples, I believe, I had ever encountered. The horn, signed by Jacob Blevins and dated 1883, had been scraped thin, and Oscar said: "Now, hold it up between you and the light and you can tell how much powder's in it." And he was right.

"Now Grandpa (Jake) he was born over here on Parched Corn, then he moved down here to Station Camp and when Grandpa died (all his brothers had married off and left) and they's nobody at home to plow for his mother and his two old maid sisters; so he moved in and lived with them".

AND THIS WAS THE GUN THAT JACOB MADE AND USED FOR MOST OF HIS LIFE?

"Yeah, yeah, that's grandpap's old hog rifle. He made it and he used it. And I used it too. Lord, I don't know at the squirrel's I've killed with it."

Jake Blevins is shown here with his wife Viannah and his two sisters, Elitha and Nancy. (Photo courtesy of Oscar Blevins)

Oscar Blevins keeps a critical eye on his grandfather's long Kentucky rifle, and on the writer also, as the latter attempts to steady the long, heavy piece. The black powder enthusiasts will not forgive me for not measuring the length of the barrel; but I don't believe I have seen a longer one. (Photo by Gary Hamilton)

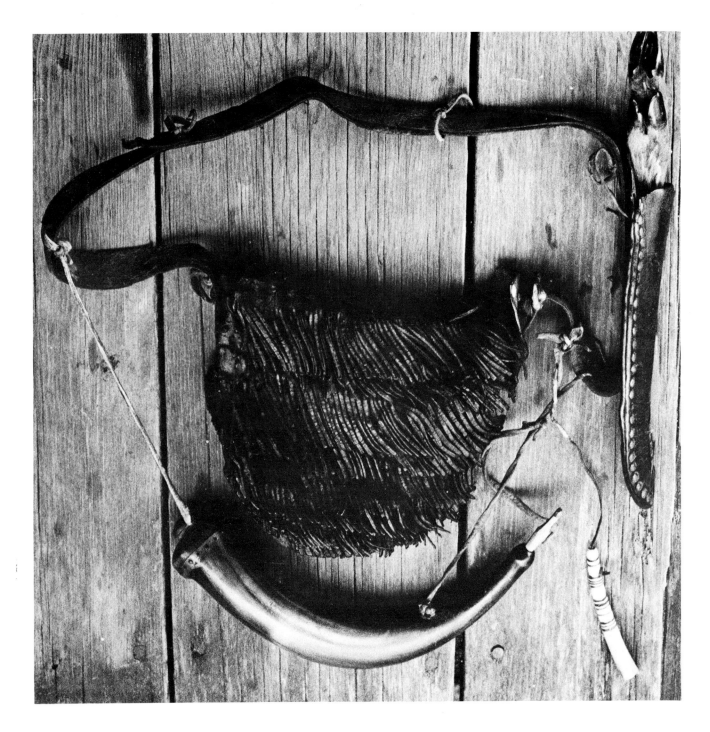

These Kentucky rifle accessories, made and used by Oscar's grandfather Jake Blevins, are, I believe, the finest I have found. The hunting bag is covered with narrow strips of leather, which serves to repel the rain and snow as well as to add aesthetic qualities. The graceful powder horn is scraped paper thin so that the powder may be seen through the transparent horn. It is signed by Jake and dated 1883. The decorated charger is made of bone. (Photo by Gary Hamilton)

INDEX